FROM COURTSHIP
TO COURTROOM

What Divorce Law
Is Doing To Marriage...

by Jed H. Abraham

Bloch Publishing Company, Inc.
New York, New York

Library of Congress Cataloging-in-Publication Data

Abraham, Jed H.
From courtship to courtroom : what divorce law is doing to marriage / by Jed H. Abraham.
   p. cm.
Includes bibliographical references.
ISBN 0-8197-0694-9 (cloth). - - ISBN 0-8197-0692-2 (pbk.)
   1. Divorce–Law and legislation–United States Popular works.
2. Divorced men–Legal status, laws, etc.–United States Popular
   works. 3. Divorce–United States Popular works. I. Title.
KF535.z9A27 1999
346.7301'66–dc21   99-42598
                                                  CIP

Book design by Rivanne, Brooklyn

Printed in the United States of America

AUTHOR'S NOTE

This book provides information and opinions about divorce law, its development, and current practice. It is not a technical legal treatise, and it does not provide legal or other professional advice. For legal advice or counsel, the reader should personally consult a competent member of the bar. Due to the dynamic nature of family law, some of the information contained in this book may require updating.

Although this book adverts to statistical and social science studies for some background information and data, the reader should understand that those kinds of studies in family law may be flawed by sampling and other technical deficiencies as well as by preconceptions about policy changes considered desirable by their authors. They can, in any case, give scant instruction in the principles and values that should guide family law, and they should always be received with appropriate caution.

To my parents David and Florence K. Abraham
of blessed memory

TABLE OF CONTENTS

ACKNOWLEDGEMENTS

"You should write a book!" she would say.

My mother was happily married for 49 years. After my father died, she spent several months a year with me reveling in the role of Grandma to my kids. An avid reader until her death at age 91, she would listen in disbelief to my doleful tales of the divorce wars. She thought they should be written up for everyone to whom they might make a difference.

"Make it short and to the point," she would insist. "Tell the men that maybe they shouldn't get married anymore!"

As the manuscript took shape, she became my editor. Whenever I lapsed into legalese, she would mark up the turgid prose for oblivion. We went through many drafts. It took me a long time to learn how to write to pass the Grandma test.

Alas, I lost her before we finished. Fortunately, her presence will always radiate from the lines I like best.

To my son Jeremy, I owe the title; to my sons Josh and Jon, the subtitle.

To Joel E. Abramson, Esq., Professor Jeff Atkinson, Asa Baber, Joshua Holo, Professor Ephraim Isaac, Sam Judlo, Bob Seidenberg, Jeffrey Stuart Shapiro, Esq., Joshua Sklare, Rabbi Moshe Soloveichik,

Deborah Steinberg Shimansky, and literary agent Elizabeth Ziemska, I am grateful for their many thoughtful comments and criticisms. The book has been immeasurably improved by their input.

To Maria Dering, I am thankful for her keen grammatical, syntactical, and stylistic suggestions.

To Amy R. Feigenbaum, I offer heartfelt appreciation for her felicitous book design.

And last, but certainly not least, to my publisher, Charles Bloch, I am indebted for his courage in publishing so politically incorrect a book. His only condition was that I tell it like it is.

PREFACE

If you're like most men, you're married, or you hope to marry some day. You think you deserve to live happily ever after, but if things don't work out that way, you'll get a civilized divorce and move on. You'll stay pals with your ex, and you'll see your kids as often as you want.

You have no idea what you're getting into.

In the fifty states and sundry territories of these United States, approximately a million men get divorced every year. That's about half the number who marry.

I know their stories. I am a divorce lawyer and mediator. Some of them call me for help, others just to get it off their chests. If you're like most men, you'll want to know their stories too, because one day their stories might be your story.

In this book, I sketch case-situations that show how divorce law has undermined marriage for men. It goes without saying, however, that in this diverse land there will always be cases that go the other way. So, when I write in the pages ahead that "the court will...," or "the law is...," I assume you will understand that I don't mean "the court always will...," or "the law everywhere is...." I do mean that these kinds of cases recur in various jurisdictions—and that you stand a significant risk of being the next case.

Not everything I describe in this book will unfailingly befall you. And if divorce law in your state happens to be more balanced than most, your risk may be lower than usual. But since divorce law tends generally to cater to women at the expense of men, and since you can never be sure where you'll be when you divorce, you should never say, "It can't happen here."

I want to stress that this book is about bad law, not bad judges or bad lawyers—or bad wives.

There are, of course, bad judges, and they're the plague. But truth be told, there are also good judges who agonize over difficult cases with the wisdom of Solomon and the forbearance of Job. As in any profession, the bench is composed of the good, the bad, and the decent. The problem is that they all work within a system of law that constrains them to do harm as well as good. So, when I take a swipe at judges and courts, I intend it as a shorthand lament that, in the current legal environment, even decent jurists may end up doing bad things to good people just by following the law.

Likewise, lawyers. Lazy and lousy lawyers are the bane of the divorce bar, but the overriding problem is not too many bad apples, but too many worms, too many bad laws for even decent lawyers to do anything about.

The same holds true, too, for wives—but with a twist. Divorce law plays off married couples as adversaries; it expects they will get champion attorneys to realize their rights. Attorneys are trained to fight hard for their clients. These ingredients, when mixed with the heightened emotions of shame, rage, fear, and vengefulness, that accompany virtually all contested divorces, place implacable pressure on the fragile virtues of modesty, restraint, politeness, and accommodation.

But there is another, unique ingredient in this witches' brew: the women's movement. For two generations now, a culturally triumphant feminism has validated the movement of married women away from homemaking and into the workplace, all the while successfully characterizing traditional marriage as the creation of evil, patriarchal men intent on repressing women. Many women, even women who would not consider themselves feminists, have internalized these attitudes, while many men, even men who pay lip service to feminist ideals, have not. When a consciousness-raised female marries an unreconstructed male, she brings to the marriage a severely compromised commitment, while he brings ancestral attitudes that automatically aggravate her ambivalence. When she turns to divorce law for an out, she is welcomed by an array of economic and social incentives that encourage her to proceed. This amplification of women's propensity to divorce may well account for virtually the entire doubling of the divorce rate since the 1960s. It seems also to account, at least in part, for the uncharacteristically bad things that otherwise good women do to decent men.

During the course of your divorce, you may be sorely tempted to alter your naturally positive view of women. You may also want to change your lawyer and your judge. I hope that, after reading this book, you'll want even more to change the law.

Jed H. Abraham

YOUR DIVORCE

The odds are 50% that your marriage will end in divorce.

The odds are 70% that your divorce will be filed by your wife.

The odds are 80% that your wife will get custody of your children—plus child support, alimony and/or a hefty chunk of your property.

From the moment your wife files for divorce, the State, acting through the court, will assert authority over everything you own. The court can then give a major share to your wife by applying the law of "equitable distribution."

The law of equitable distribution is based on the "partnership theory of marriage." This theory holds that your marriage is a business partnership. Everything you earned during marriage you earned for the partnership. Therefore, upon divorce, all your accumulated assets must be split "equitably" between you and your "partner."

The theory also holds that if the property your ex is awarded at divorce doesn't yield enough to support her at the standard of living you established during the marriage, then you should "equitably" pay her the difference in alimony until she becomes self-supporting—in most states, even if the breakdown of the marriage was her fault.

The partnership theory of marriage doesn't quite cover everything you made during marriage: it doesn't cover your children.

Even though you and your ex were partners in the creation of your children, and even though you each contributed "equitably" to their upbringing, these considerations will carry little weight in court. Yielding to precedent and preconception, the court will commonly decide that it is in the "best interest" of your children to be in the sole custody of their mother.

As sole custodian, your ex will acquire primary parental authority to live with your children and to determine their general development, including their health care, education, and religious training.

You may "visit" with them on scheduled weekends.

After the court awards your ex the sole custody of your children, it will award you something very special also. It will award you the obligation to pay child support.

Your child support obligation will not be determined by your children's basic needs. The court will first calculate your income, which it will then proceed to tax at a predetermined "guideline" rate set by law. The guideline rate will vary according to the number of your children. It may also vary according to your income level and that of your wife.

At your child support hearing, you'll be permitted to introduce evidence that the guideline rate is too high—that it will generate more money than is needed by your children or that it will leave you with too little to live on. But the law strongly presumes that the guideline rate produces the correct *minimum* amount of child support. The burden of proof will be on you to overcome this presumption. The court won't reduce your guideline rate, except in extreme circumstances.

If you are a wage earner, the child support you owe will be withheld from your wages and paid directly to your ex without your ever having to write her a check.

Once in the clutches of the child support system, you'll be systematically shorn of your economic autonomy.

• If you lose your job, you must continue to pay the court-ordered amount. To get relief, you must file a petition with the court. You may also have to hire a lawyer to argue the petition—which precisely now you would be hard-pressed to do.

In court, you won't get complete relief. Initially, the court will expect you to pay a large part of the ordered amount out of savings. It will expect you to reduce your own standard of living before it reduces your child support obligation. You'll also have to pay any amounts you failed to pay from the day you lost your job until the day you filed your petition. In full.

• If you find a new job which pays less than your old one, the court needn't reduce your child support obligation correspondingly. The court may suspect that you took the lower-paying job to reduce your child support payments. The burden will be on you to prove you didn't.

• If you leave your job to start your own business, and you pay yourself a minimal salary until the business prospers, the court needn't grant you child support relief. It may lecture you about "putting your children first."

• If you remarry and have children with your new wife, the court needn't grant you child support relief. It may lecture you again, this time about not bringing more children into the world when you already have children enough to support. And if your new wife works, the court may look at her income as an indirect source of more child support.

• In the meantime, your ex may claim that your children's needs have increased significantly, and she'll seek to increase your payments.

You will have to prove that you can't afford the increase. It won't be enough to show that your income hasn't increased significantly. If it has, your ex needn't show that the children's needs have increased correspondingly.

• If your wages are not withheld and you fail to pay your child support, the State will garnish your pay, slap liens on your property, intercept your tax refunds, report you to credit agencies, discontinue your driver's license, suspend your professional and business permits, hold you in contempt of court, put your face on a wanted poster, throw you in jail, and deny you food stamps. But if your ex doesn't spend that very same support on the children, the State will do…nothing.

• Your child support obligation doesn't necessarily end when your children grow up, leave home, and become legally responsible adults. In many states, you may be ordered to contribute to their college tuition, their room and board, and their travel expenses, even though married parents can't be ordered to pay for these things.

You may also owe your ex one further payment: part or all of her "reasonable" attorney's fees.

The court will try to eliminate any financial advantage you have in selecting a lawyer. It will not make her fritter away her equitable share of your property on something so inequitable as her attorney's fees.

It will make you fritter away your share.

Equitable distribution, alimony, and child support law produce a net transfer of assets from you to your ex.

Child custody law produces a net transfer of custody from you to your ex.

From an economic point of view, divorce is a wealth redistribution racket that forces fathers to make payments to mothers. From a social point of view, it is a family resocialization scheme that turns mothers into State-sponsored single parents and fathers into infrequent visitors of their estranged children.

When the economic and the social aspects of divorce law are netted, fathers are two-time losers. They must pay for the maintenance of women to whom they are no longer married and for the support of children to whom they are no longer fully parents—all the while having to carry the costs of their own new households.

This skewed regime spawns strong reactionary forces. The strife which the divorce should have ended has only just begun.

Your ex will warm to calling all the shots. She may cancel your visitation now and then. If she's truly mean-spirited, she'll go much further. Under the cover of her court-appointed role as sole custodian, she'll systematically sever your relationship with the children. She'll badmouth you to them. She'll schedule their extracurricular activities during your visitation time. For good measure, she may accuse you of domestic violence and child abuse.

The authorities will act quickly to "protect" your children from you. They'll curtail your visitation during their investigation; you'll be restricted to being with your children only in the presence of a supervisor, and you'll be ordered to pay the supervisor's fees.

In the end, your children themselves will refuse to spend any time with you. Their brainwashing will be complete and irreversible. They will be alienated from you forever.

More efficiently, your ex may simply move with the children to a distant community, with the law's acquiescence.

As the struggle wears on, your frustrations will deepen. You'll pass up overtime work rather than earn extra income for your ex. You'll be tempted to "do a fade": to flee the jurisdiction, and disappear.

Your health will deteriorate. Your sleep will be disturbed. You'll feel fatigued and distracted. You'll sweat a lot. You'll develop elusive internal pain. The tests will rule out a tumor, the pills will help a little. But the pain won't go away.

While the law pits your ex against you, its ultimate victims will be your children. Your boys will be battered by the absence of their most important role model. Your girls will be gutted by the loss of their primary standard for opposite-sex comportment.

They'll seek compensation elsewhere—in aggressive, seductive, or rebellious behavior. They'll develop deep-seated psychological problems. They'll drop out of school, lose their jobs, and get into trouble with the police.

You'll know no peace for a generation.

* * *

The odds are even that your marriage will end in divorce.

The odds are daunting that your divorce will disrupt your well-being. You'll lose your children and your property. You'll pay alimony, child support and attorneys' fees. You'll be subject to State scrutiny over employment and spending decisions. You'll have chronic health problems. You'll watch helplessly as your children carry seething emotional scars into adulthood.

The odds are it doesn't pay for you to marry and have kids.

PART ONE

HOW DIVORCE LAW
TAKES AWAY YOUR PROPERTY

CHAPTER ONE

EQUITABLE DISTRIBUTION IN THEORY

"Equitable distribution" is a deceptive term. It suggests that other forms of property distribution are not equitable. The truth is that equitable distribution itself is not equitable. It's a legal fiction that lets the court seize your property and give it to your ex.

It works like this: During marriage, the property you acquire is considered yours, as if you were single. Come your divorce, however, and everything changes. The law says that your ex had an invisible interest in your property that suddenly becomes visible when you get divorced. Even though you can't recall ever giving it to her.

It wasn't always so.

Under the late common law that prevailed just before equitable distribution, your wife had no rights to your property. At divorce, you generally kept your property, and she kept hers. If it would be clearly unfair for you to keep your property—say your ex worked regularly in your business but didn't take a salary—the court would give her a "special equity," a compensatory share in the value of your business.

Usually, your ex's needs were addressed by a court order requiring you to pay her periodic alimony—for life, or until her remarriage. If your income were erratic or otherwise did not suffice to fund these payments, the court, in some states, would look to your property for a supplement.

The common law system was based on traditional notions of marriage and family. The marriage contract created an enduring and hallowed bond grounded in mutual fidelity, which, if breached, demanded redress. The State, which had sanctioned the marriage contract, would not lightly tolerate its dissolution.

To secure a divorce—an undoing of the marriage contract— a spouse had to prove that the other spouse was at "fault," that he or she had committed an outrageous act, such as adultery, that thoroughly undermined the marriage.

If the husband was at fault, he was ordered to compensate his wife for the breakdown of the marriage: his duty to support her was carried over after the divorce as alimony. If the wife was at fault, her husband was relieved of his marital duty to support her. She was not ordered to compensate him for his loss of the domestic service that she was duty-bound to render in exchange for his support.

The common law developed during that bygone era when both men and women expected husbands to be providers and wives to be homemakers. Legal separation and divorce—but not necessarily marital discord—were uncommon. With rare exception, when they did occur, they were stigmatized.

Over the course of this century, these conditions—which were already coming into conflict with America's growing ethos of individualism—changed radically. Medical advances lengthened life expectancies and enabled family planning. Wives began to expect and experience long periods of childlessness. At the same time, technology drastically reduced the time-consuming burdens of homemaking, while employment opportunities in the clerical, service, and professional sectors of the economy grew at the expense of heavy industry and farming.

Wives reacted to these changes by entering the paid workforce in record numbers. Although men generally earned more than women, working wives increasingly vied with their husbands for a role as provider. Correspondingly, they began to expect their husbands to assume homemaking tasks. Sexual equality became the political ideal. Feminists embraced this model and lobbied for the repeal of sex-based, discriminatory standards in the workplace. The labor market responded by dropping its assumption that a husband should earn a "family wage," and the real income of men plummeted.

Many traditional marriages could not withstand this pressure. The divorce rate soared, and the stigma of divorce virtually disappeared.

In the wake of these trends, the common law notion of personal fault as the basis for a divorce action appeared altogether archaic and unseemly. Besides, fault was commonly fabricated to satisfy legal requirements. The staging of an "adultery" became a regular act in certain divorce lawyers' repertoires. In some states, fault was deftly defined down to include tenuous instances of "mental cruelty" and relatively short periods of voluntary separation.

Then, in 1970, California entirely eliminated fault from its law. It required merely a showing that the marriage had irretrievably broken down. Similar "no-fault" statutes soon swept the country. They permitted a divorce even if one spouse simply wanted out of the marriage.

With the demise of fault, the theoretical basis for alimony—the standard relief for a divorcing wife—collapsed. Why should a husband who had not undermined the marriage be forced to continue to support his ex-wife?

The solution to this problem was found in the handful of southern and western states that had previously adopted a "community property" legal system. Under community property law, a marriage creates an economic partnership or "community" of spouses. All property acquired by the spouses' efforts is acquired by the community. The spouses are equal partners in the community. If the wife earns less than the husband, the wife's "homemaker contribution"—her imputed contribution to the household economy—is implicitly capitalized into a per capita share of the community's value.

Community property law was transferred to common law states, but with one major modification: it would come into effect only upon divorce. During marriage, each spouse would continue to own his or her property separately. Only in the event of divorce would the concept of community property (now called "marital property") kick in. And then, in most states, the court was empowered to give a majority, even a large majority, to one spouse based on "equitable" considerations and regardless of that spouse's marital fault.

Reformers hailed equitable distribution as a major advance in divorce law. It replaced a series of small alimony payments spread out over many years—which might be interrupted by the death or disappearance of the husband—with a large, immediate, certain, lump sum amount. And if the property transferred to the wife turned out to be inadequate to support her at the standard of living established during the marriage, the court could still order the husband to pay alimony out of his income and remaining property, until she acquired sufficient marketable skills to support herself.

The fact that equitable distribution imposed a new system of law retroactively did not rattle the reformers. They were enthralled by the opportunity to eliminate the legacy of fault from the divorce process and by the new public policy of sexual equality. It was only fair that husbands and wives should emerge on comparable economic footings after divorce, which would reflect their presumptively comparable contributions during marriage.

Equitable distribution survived all constitutional attacks, handily.

Insensibly, however, no-fault equitable distribution began to upset the delicate socio-economic balance of the traditional marriage contract. By inflating the wife's homemaker contribution— from being the consideration for which she received the financial support of her husband into the automatic equivalent of his market labor—equitable distribution granted the wife a potential, post-divorce economic windfall. In most states, her homemaker contribution would not be offset by her "homemaker fault," her violation of the non-economic obligations of her marriage contract. So, an emotionally unsupportive or abusive wife, by no more than her imputed economic function in the household, could now assert a claim, not just for marital support, but also for some 50% of her husband's accumulated earnings, plus additional post-marital maintenance from him. Effectively, her husband was obliged to accumulate, during marriage, post-divorce property for a disloyal wife, gratis. The reciprocal dependencies of the marriage relationship, the intertwining socio-economic exchanges which, for better or for worse, worked to bind the traditional marriage together, were thus silently, but thoroughly, unravelled.

In the next chapter, I present a somewhat technical description of how equitable distribution law takes away your property in practice. If you don't think you'd be interested in the details, please skip the next chapter and go on to how custody law takes away your children.

CHAPTER TWO

EQUITABLE DISTRIBUTION
IN PRACTICE

In actual practice, equitable distribution is a crazy-quilt. What is "equitable" in one state is not quite equitable in another. What you get to keep after your divorce will depend on where you live.

In some states, all your property is distributable to your ex, even property you acquired before marriage. These states have moved far beyond the pretense of the "partnership theory of marriage": they don't care that your wife wasn't your "partner" before you married her. If you're married and you have property, it all goes into the marital pot.

Most states, however, allow for two categories of property: marital and non-marital. You can keep your non-marital property. The court will distribute only your marital property.

Your marital property is all the property you acquired during marriage by your personal effort. Your salary is marital property, even though only your work, and not your wife's, produced it. So is the business you singlehandedly built from scratch.

This rule, that personal effort always produces marital property, is the linchpin of equitable distribution. The State has decreed that you are not allowed during marriage to create personal wealth—formerly known as private property—unless your wife agrees. Your wife is your silent partner, and the State is your silent administrator, by law.

Property you acquire other than by personal effort—such as gifts and inheritances—is generally non-marital. But in many states, the law maintains a strong presumption that all property— even gifts and inheritances—that you acquire during marriage is marital unless you can prove it to be non-marital. The law may hold you to a heightened standard of proof. A preponderance of the evidence in your favor may not do; your proof will have to be "clear and convincing."

The bottom line of this marital property presumption is that the court will seek to decree as much of your property as possible to be marital.

Equitable distribution statutes can be vague. They don't always tell you what "property" means. They leave it to the courts to decide, after the fact, whether assets such as your pension, your business goodwill, your unexercised stock options, even your academic degrees, professional certificates and trade licenses, are the kind of "property" covered by the law.

Case law doesn't always tell you, either. Not only across state lines but also within a state, courts may differ among themselves and announce contradictory rulings. The state's supreme court, perhaps years later, has to settle the matter.

The statutes also don't always tell you what "non-marital" means. Is the rental income you earn during marriage on the three-flat you purchased before marriage marital or non-marital? Does the monthly interest on your pre-marital savings account suddenly become marital when you marry?

Depends where you live, and when.

The magical moment after which your ex begins to acquire that invisible potential ownership interest in your property— when the property you acquire is deemed marital—is usually the moment you marry. But in some states, it can even precede your marriage. If you purchase a house before you marry with the intention of using it as your marital home, it may be presumed to be marital property. This could be the result even where the statute specifically states that marital property means property acquired after the marriage.

Once your property has become marital, it will stay marital, at least until you separate. In many states, the magical moment casts its spell well after you separate and until you actually divorce. In these states, the law stoutly insists that your personal effort—your salary, your business profit—is for the ongoing benefit of your wife even after she has already separated from you, even after she has filed for divorce against you. Your wife remains your silent partner even after she has informed you—not so silently—that you are no longer her partner.

Equitable distribution law can give the court wide latitude to determine what your intentions were concerning your property. The court can decide that by using a certain amount of your non-marital property in a certain way, you intended to transform or "transmute" it into marital property.

In order to understand how this can happen, you must first understand that different states have different theories about how property becomes marital.

In many states, each component of a piece of property is sorted out to determine if it is marital or non-marital.

For example, that rental three-flat you purchased before your marriage is non-marital property. Its net value as of the date of your marriage will remain your non-marital property during the marriage. But the mortgage principal payments you make with money you earned during the marriage are marital.

So the three-flat has both marital and non-marital components. Upon divorce, you keep the non-marital component. The marital component is divided between you and your ex.

Some states take a different tack. In their view, a single piece of property must be either marital or non-marital. It cannot be both. Therefore, since your three-flat started out as non-marital, it will remain entirely your non-marital property.

But what about the funds you earned during the marriage to pay off the mortgage principal? Here, these states differ widely.

Some hold that your three-flat remains non-marital; however, the value of your marital earnings which you used to pay off the mortgage principle will be equitably distributed to both you and your ex. Others also hold your three-flat remains non-marital, but they will distribute a more than equitable share of other marital property to your ex, or award alimony to your ex as compensation. Or both.

And a few others hold that because you infused marital funds into your non-marital three-flat, you "transmuted" the three-flat entirely into marital property. The only way you can retrieve it is by convincing the court to distribute an "equitably" lopsided share back to you.

You may also trigger this drastic result by nonchalantly upgrading your non-marital three-flat with some well-meant personal effort (marital property).

You might think it reasonable that if your non-marital three-flat can be transmuted into marital property, then it can somehow be transmuted back into non-marital property.

Reasonable, but not under equitable distribution.

Say you used funds from your non-marital bank account to improve the transmuted—and now marital—three-flat. The court will not presume you intended to transmute back the three-flat into your non-marital property. Your ex will claim that your actions show you intended to make a gift of your non-marital funds to the marital estate. You'll have to prove to the court you didn't. Your sworn testimony may not be enough. It may be considered self-serving.

You might also think it reasonable that if your ex shares any gain in the value of your non-marital property due to your personal effort, she should also share any loss.

Reasonable, but not under equitable distribution.

Say you traded commodities with your non-marital inheritance and you ended up with lemons. The court won't order your ex to share the loss. Bitter lemons.

Same even if she did the trades with your inheritance.

Equitable distribution requires you to keep very detailed records. Without them, you may not be able to rebut the strong presumption that all the property you acquired during marriage is marital.

But if you're like most men, you didn't know you'd have to be a bean-counter when you got married. You didn't know you'd have to tag all your property to protect your ownership at divorce. Say you sold non-marital stocks and periodically reinvested the proceeds during marriage: if you can't trace your trades all the way back to the original non-marital stocks, your current holdings will be presumed to be marital and distributed away to your ex.

"Discovery" lies at the heart of equitable distribution.

Soon after filing for divorce, your wife will demand complete disclosure of all your business and financial dealings. She'll demand all recent tax returns, especially those filed after your separation. She'll demand all other relevant documents, no matter how confidential.

You'll be forced to complete long, detailed questionnaires. You'll be grilled intensively, under oath, by your wife's lawyer. You'll be pressed to produce mounds of personal papers.

These ordeals will consume an enormous amount of time. They'll generate fat fees to your wife's lawyer and to yours. They'll take you away from making the living you have to make in order to pay your ex, her lawyer, and yours.

After reviewing the discovered documents, your wife's lawyer may charge you with "dissipation."

The doctrine of dissipation prohibits you from spending marital money on matters not related to the marriage after the marriage has begun to break down. It's designed to conserve marital property so that the court can give it away to your ex.

Funding a new trust for your children's college education is dissipation; so, too, is paying your mother's emergency medical bills, unless, of course, your wife gives you prior permission.

Conversely, if you purposely work less and reduce your income so as not to produce marital property for your wife during your divorce, that's also dissipation.

When you are accused of dissipating "missing" property, the burden shifts to you to prove you didn't dissipate. If the court finds that you did, it will add the dissipated amount back into the marital pot as a phantom value and then distribute the phantom value to you. That is, the court will count as part of your share of the marital property the funds it found you to have spent already.

A gambling binge or a stock market fling to which your wife objected and which resulted in losses is dissipation. You will get the losses as part of your share of the marital property. But your wins are marital property. Your ex will get her equitable share of them in addition to her share of your other property. Heads she wins, tails she wins, too.

Before your marital property can be distributed by the court, it must be valued. This presents little problem in the case of cash, bank accounts, and traded securities. Some properties, however, don't have easily ascertainable values. Small businesses, professional practices, antiques, even the family home have to be appraised before their values can be ascertained.

Valuation, in the absence of an active market, is largely a matter of opinion. Professional appraisers purport to approximate a property's value, but there is often no independent way to verify an appraiser's opinion.

The court will be presented with conflicting appraisals. Your appraiser's will favor your position. Your wife's will favor hers. The court will likely make an evidentiary finding somewhere between the difference. The difference could be substantial.

The court's valuation has to be as of a specific date. Some states require that it be the date of trial, others set it as the date of divorce, while still others fix it somewhere between the date of separation and the date of divorce.

Unforeseeable events can occur between the date of valuation and the date of actual distribution. On October 19, 1987, the stock market crashed. If you were ordered to give your ex a cash settlement by October 31, 1987, based on the valuation of your stockholdings as of September 1, 1987—the date of your divorce—you likely experienced a big loss. Of course, the market could have gone up instead, and you could have experienced a big gain. But this is your divorce.

Some property is almost impossible to value. The court will try, anyway. In states that consider professional degrees to be marital property, the court will calculate from the conflicting appraisals a value that represents "the present value of the future worth" of your dental career. It will then order you to pay a share of that value to your ex, either in a lump sum or in installments. Since this is a property division as of a specific date, it cannot be altered later.

Of course, an appraiser can't predict the specific professional success of anyone. At best, he can produce statistical averages and venture a guess about the probabilities that someone will conform to the averages. He can be wrong more often than right. But this won't be apparent until many years after the appraisal.

So, if your dental career was valued by the court before the fluoridation of your local water supply reduced the number of your patients' cavities, you gave your ex more than you were worth, and there won't be enough cavities for you to fill to make up for the one you just filled.

* * *

In most states, the court does not have to divide marital property equally—only equitably, and it has enormous discretion to determine what "equitably" is. Its decision will not be reversed unless an appellate court can be persuaded that no reasonable person could have rendered such a decision. In virtually identical cases, a decision by one court to divide the marital property 60/40, and a decision by a different court to divide it 40/60 could both be upheld by the same appellate court as reasonable and, therefore, "equitable."

Equitable distribution statutes set forth certain "factors" that the court must consider when it exercises its discretion. These factors include:

Who contributed how much to the acquisition of the property?

What was the wife's homemaker contribution to the marriage?

How long did the marriage last?

Who gets custody of the children?

Who has the greater ability to earn income in the future?

How much non-marital property does each spouse have?

Applying these factors, the court could "equitably" divide marital property by giving most of it to the spouse who didn't earn it. The fact that you earned all the marital property may be overcome by the court's estimate of your wife's homemaker contribution and its award to her of the custody of the children. If you happen also to have a well-paying job and a lot of non-marital property, the court's decision will be easier still.

It's irrelevant that most of these factors have nothing to do with the production of the specific property actually being distributed. The court must do "equity" with all your property.

* * *

Equitable distribution creates a strong incentive to cave in to a "rambo"—an abusive wife's attorney. Better to pay up now than go through the torment of an intensive discovery and the torture of an extended trial. Better to cut your loses now than pay more in attorney's fees and time off from work later. Better to settle now than risk an off-the-wall decision by the court...

PART TWO

HOW DIVORCE LAW
TAKES AWAY YOUR CHILDREN

CHAPTER THREE

THE "BEST INTEREST OF THE CHILD"

The law of equitable distribution expropriates your property for distribution to your ex. But at least it lets you keep some for yourself. After all, the law of equitable distribution is "equitable."

The law of child custody is not. No equitable doctrine protects your relationship with your children. The only equitable consideration before the court in a custody case is the "best interest" of the children. In practice, the best interest of the children means whatever the court, in its "sound discretion," decides it to mean. Predominantly, the court will decide it means that your children should be put in the custody of your ex. The sole custody of your ex.

When the court awards sole custody to your ex, you lose some basic rights of parenthood: You lose the right to decide where your children go to school. You lose the right to choose their doctors. You lose the right to direct their primary religious training.

Worst of all, you lose the right to reside with them; you are granted instead a limited "entitlement" to "visit" with them.

It wasn't always so.

During the eighteenth and early nineteenth centuries, the father was the undisputed head of his household. He was responsible for its financial support as well as for its moral and civic integrity. He was also expected to take an active role in the upbringing and education of his children.

His custody was exclusive and conclusive. He did not share it with the mother and it could not be taken away from him unless he grossly mistreated the children. Even upon his death, he could delegate it by will, in the absence of which the court would appoint guardians for the children. In the rare event of divorce, the law naturally expected the father to continue as custodian. There were limited exceptions in the cases of alcoholic, dissolute, or "immoral" fathers.

During the last half of the nineteenth century and into the twentieth century, fathers experienced a dramatic decline in parental status. Industrialization, with its stark separation of home and workplace, and child labor laws, which reduced apprenticeship opportunities, severed the traditional mentoring nexus between fathers and children. Away for long hours earning a living for their families, fathers lost touch with the daily rhythm of their children's lives. As mothers moved in to fill the breach, it was left for fathers to enforce the discipline dictated by mothers. The faraway father and the smothering mother soon became the staple scapegoats of the newfound, fashionable field of psychology.

With its emphasis on the primacy of the mother-child bond, psychological theory seemed to make good common sense. Courts began to find that the mother should naturally obtain custody upon the father's death. States began to legislate that, even during marriage, the mother should at least share custody of her children jointly with the father. As divorce became more common, it seemed to make good common sense, too, that the children should remain with the parent to whom they had psychologically "bonded" more closely: the mother.

The old common law rule that the children should remain with the father appeared altogether arbitrary and ill-conceived. Children were women's work. Mom and the kids needed each other. Dad's deed was already done. That was how God made us. In a chorus of self-congratulatory enlightenment, courts across the country impiously swept away the ancient precedent of paternal custody. In its stead, they introduced the "tender years doctrine"—later reformulated in gender-neutral terms as the "best interest of the child standard"—which favored sole maternal custody, especially for young children.

Courts did not formally frame these new concepts as the novelties they were. They camouflaged their innovations by claiming they were exercising their long-established, surrogate prerogatives as the *parens patriae*, the ultimate sovereign father, the Big Daddy, of all the children of the realm.

This legal legerdemain, however, served only to pervert *parens patriae* along with paternal custody. For the doctrine of *parens patriae* was originally conceived to allow the court to appoint a guardian to conserve and administer the inheritance of a minor child whose father had died. In the absence of his father, the child had no legal capacity. The *parens patriae* guardian was commissioned to act in the "best interest" of his ward. Never was it a goal of *parens patriae* to substitute a guardian for a competent living father.

Nevertheless, the majesty of the term was irresistible, all the more so because it implied a stirring mandate to act in the "best

interest" of the children who so clearly needed the ongoing ministrations of their mothers. And so it was that a doctrine designed
to provide a surrogate father to an orphaned child came to be
used to rationalize the orphaning of a child from his living father.

There was another thorn in the theory: granted, Mom and the
kids needed each other more than either needed Dad—but they
also needed Dad's paycheck. They ate Mom's bread, but they lived
on Dad's dough. The *parens patriae* that originally served to protect a minor from economic hardship was now threatening to
cause it. So after relieving him of his parental rights and dispatch-
ing him from active fatherhood, the court briefly retrieved Dad
and ordered him to pay child support to Mom.

Just as the law finally got it right, economic and social forces
again began to press in other directions. The industrial economy
opened up to women, mothers flocked to the workplace, and the
divorce rate skyrocketed.

Fathers soon learned to retaliate against their court-ordered
loss of custody. Many refused to pay their court-ordered child
support. Some "kidnapped" the children. A few shot the judge.

Psychologists soon got around to noticing the importance of
fathers. Evidence accumulated that children, even infants, bond
to fathers as well as to mothers. Surveys disclosed that fathers are
as competent as mothers to be caretakers of children. Studies
indicated the need for both parents to remain closely involved
with their children after divorce. Statistics showed that the few
fathers who got to share custodial arrangements with their ex-
wives were exceptionally reliable child support payers. Research
revealed that children raised in single-mother households fared
no better on a variety of psycho/socio-economic measurements

than children from single-father homes. Doubts were raised about the constitutionality of denying custody to fit fathers solely on the basis of their sex.

As lawmakers fidgeted with divorce property law, small groups of fathers across the county began to press for changes in custody law. They noted that, during marriage, parents share the custody of their children. They emphasized that, at divorce, parents divorce only each other, not their children. The court, therefore, had no reason to choose between two fit, divorcing parents and make only one the custodian. The children still need both parents, at divorce more than ever. The parents—both parents— still love and still need their children, too.

In 1979, California, following fledgling attempts in other states, passed the first comprehensive post-divorce joint custody statute. It empowered the court to award custody to both parents, jointly. Today, some 45 states have statutes allowing some degree of joint custody.

For all this legal change, however, the change in practice was surprisingly moderate. Although some states made joint custody the preferred statutory outcome, many courts around the country did not look favorably upon the new joint custody laws. Judges who believed that children belong with their mothers didn't change their minds just because the law now said they could. Two decades after joint custody first became law, some 80% of divorcing mothers still come out of court with effective sole custody of their children firmly in hand.

Most courts award only "joint legal custody," not "joint physical custody." Joint legal custody is the authority for you to share in making major decisions about your children's welfare: education, health care, religious training. Joint physical custody is the authority for you to reside with your children for a substantial percentage—close to 50%—of the time. If you are awarded joint legal custody without joint physical custody, the time you are allowed to be with your children is generally no greater than it would be if your ex were awarded sole legal and physical custody and you were awarded no custody.

In a dispute between joint legal custodians, courts tend to side with the one who has physical custody. They consider her to be the "real" custodian. Deep down, they believe that joint legal custody that is not coupled with joint physical custody is just a placebo, a kind of custodial consolation prize that has little compelling content. This is a very bitter pill for the many divorced fathers who fight for joint legal custody only to find they are still less than full-fledged parents to their children, by court order.

CHAPTER FOUR

WHEN YOUR WIFE FILES
FOR DIVORCE

When your wife files for divorce, she will likely petition for "temporary" custody of the children and for "temporary" alimony and child support. Simultaneously, she may claim that the marital tension you are generating around the house is jeopardizing the well-being of the children, and she will petition the court to evict you from the family home.

You may continue to pay the bills from your quarters in exile.

If your wife cannot prove that your presence in the home is jeopardizing the children, she may make a more serious claim. She may charge you with committing an act of physical or emotional "abuse" against her or the children. Under the state's domestic violence statute, she will not have to prove that you actually abused anyone; she will only have to "make averments sufficient to indicate" that you did. She will not even have to notify you that she has accused you. She can simply go to court "ex parte," without you or your lawyer to defend you, and get an "emergency" order of protection to evict you.

It will not matter that you're a joint owner of your home. It will not matter that you're the sole owner of your home. It will not matter that your home is entirely your non-marital property. You will be summarily evicted from your home without a hearing on your wife's accusation that you're an abuser.

After your eviction, you may petition the court for a full, adversarial rehearing. But if, as is common, there are no other witnesses, your case will hinge on whether the court believes you or your wife. If it believes you, it risks being wrong and that you will commit abuse again; if it believes your wife, it risks being wrong and that you will be unjustly deprived of the use of your property. It does not take a judge to know which risk is easier to take.

Having succeeded in one fell swoop to snatch exclusive possession of your home and your children, your wife will control the momentum of the case.

Your life will now cascade into chaos. Your wife will have withdrawn the balances from your joint account. You will be living in a small room in a cheap motel. Your personal belongings will still be in the house. Your friends will stop talking to you when they hear about the abuse charge.

You will wonder what your boss will do when he hears about it.

You will need a lawyer.

You will ask the men at the pub if they know a good divorce lawyer. When they stop laughing, they'll tell you. They'll tell you to run away. Far away. They'll tell you that, if you stay and fight, you'll lose everything; that your wife, your lawyer and your wife's lawyer will win it all.

You think your case will be different. You are a good father. You work hard to provide for your kids. You play with them when you get home from work. You take them fishing on weekends, you take them to root for the home teams. You help them with their homework, you read to them before they go to sleep, you tell them funny stories.

The men will tell you that none of that counted in their cases. What counted was that their wives were at home more than they were and that their wives were the mothers of their children.

You think your case will be different. Your wife unloads the kids on you the moment you get home from work, and they're all yours till you tuck them in. When they were younger, you—not your wife—got up at night. You hugged them when they cried, you changed their diapers, you gave them their bottles, and you waited till they drifted back to sleep.

The men will remind you that your wife is still the mother of your children.

You think your case will be different. Your wife is curt with the kids, and she whacks them when they get out of line.

The men will remind you that your wife is still at home more than you are.

You think your case will be different. Your wife is at home more because she has only a part-time job. She got it just to get away from the kids, and it costs more in taxes and baby-sitters than it's worth. She says she wants to work, but she won't go out and get a real job. She's a lousy housekeeper, she cooks out of cans, and she spends half the time on the phone with her friends.

The men will remind you that you heard it first from them to run away.

* * *

The lawyer will tell you he's handled many cases like yours. He'll tell you he was able to help his clients. But it cost them money. It'll cost you money too. He cannot tell you exactly how much because he'll charge you by the hour: $200 an hour. His retainer will be $7,500, up front. He'll tell you there are divorce lawyers who charge less, but you only get you what you pay for. And how much are your kids worth, anyway?

He will tell you he can negotiate you out of the abuse charge. You'll have to stay out of the house, give your wife temporary legal custody of the children, and pay her temporary child support, but the abuse charge will be dropped and you'll be allowed to pick up the children and take them for a visit every other Sunday afternoon for five full hours. This arrangement will be approved by an order of the court.

On the other hand, if you want to fight the abuse charge and try to get back into the house, the retainer will be $15,000 and court time will be $250 an hour. Then, there are the fees of the other lawyers you may have to hire. Your wife might bring her case to the district attorney, which may result in a criminal indictment against you. She might also file a damage claim in civil court. So you'll need a criminal lawyer to defend you against the indictment and a personal injury lawyer to defend you against the damage charge.

You may also have to hire a mental health professional as an expert witness on your behalf. Before the hearing, he'll put your whole family through a battery of psychological tests. He'll also interview everybody, most likely more than once.

You can also expect a petition from your wife for her attorney's fees. Since your wife is a mother with only a part-time job, and you earn considerably more than she does, the court will grant at least part of her petition. You'll then be in the position of financing your wife's abuse charge against you.

You will mutter to the lawyer that you just want to clear your name. If you settle the abuse charge and agree to stay away from the house, it's like agreeing to punishment for something you didn't do.

The lawyer will explain that the odds are against you. If your wife can give any kind of evidence that the judge can hang his hat on—if she can convince him that you harassed, or even just threatened to harass—her, he will feel pressure to grant her petition. For an order of protection, he doesn't need proof beyond a reasonable doubt; he only needs a <u>preponderance of the evidence</u> and an impression that she is more credible than you.

If you lose on the abuse charge, you jeopardize the whole custody case. And then it may be on to the criminal and civil damage cases. Better to settle the abuse charge now as best you can and get it dismissed, at least for the interim; then, figure out how to deal with it later if your wife tries to raise it again when you seek permanent custody. At least, you won't have to litigate it twice.

So, with the money I just saved you, go get yourself a decent place to live, even if you can't afford it. You'll have to show the court that the kids can live comfortably with you.

And in the meantime, you can collect your personal belongings from the house—when your children aren't home.

You will purchase peace by settling the abuse charge. The price you pay will become apparent only later.

Your children will wonder why you left home. Mommy may not tell them the truth. She may tell them that you did bad things and you had to go away.

Your children will be very scared. They won't believe Mommy at first. They'll believe that you went away because *they* did bad things, that you're angry with them and don't want to live with them anymore.

During your first visitation, you'll tell your children why you left home. You won't tell them the truth, either. You won't tell them that Mommy forced you out to achieve a tactical advantage in her divorce case. You'll tell them that you and Mommy hadn't been getting along and that you and Mommy agreed it would be better if you left the house for a while. You'll assure them you still love them very much.

Your children won't believe you. They'll want to know why you left, and not Mommy. They'll see that you're not angry with them, but they'll sense that you're nervous about what happened and that you seem to be hiding something.

They will believe that maybe Mommy was right after all.

As the weeks roll by, you'll miss the children more and more. The fortnight between your Sunday visitations will seem like an eternity. The five hours you have for each visitation will seem like a fleeting instant. You'll spend a lot of the time in the car just picking them up, shuttling them around, and bringing them back. There will be no opportunity to be natural, to do the everyday things you used to do with them at home.

The children won't be happy either. They'll walk impassively from the house to your waiting car; they'll know better than to show Mommy that they look forward to seeing you. Once with you, they'll unwind. But just as they get used to being with you, it'll be time to return. They'll become agitated and then subdued as they slump out of the car and put on the mask of indifference they wore at the beginning.

* * *

Sometimes you won't get to see your children on visitation. When you arrive, they won't be ready. You'll get out of the car and irritably ring the bell. Your wife will tell you through the locked door that the children are playing at their friends' houses. They don't want to come back just now.

Sometimes the children won't be playing at their friends' houses. They'll be playing on extracurricular sports teams whose schedules happen to coincide with your visitation.

Sometimes the children won't be playing on their teams. They'll be watching a video. No, your wife won't interrupt their video for your visitation; they don't want to go with you now. No, she won't agree to make-up time next Sunday.

Sometimes you'll get to see your children for visitation, and you'll wish you hadn't. They'll sit sullenly in the car and rebuff all your efforts to entertain them. They'll tell you they wanted to go to their friend's birthday party which Mommy was helping to chaperone, but Mommy made them go with you even though they didn't want to.

At first, you'll phone them every day. They'll tell you about school and what they did with their friends. You'll help them figure out a math problem or tell them the meaning of a new word. But soon your calls will be answered by an answering machine. You'll leave messages, but the children won't call back. You'll leave an irate message for your wife that she should give the kids your messages. She'll call you right back and threaten to reinstate the abuse charge if you don't stop harassing her over the phone. And she won't make the children call you back if they don't want to.

* * *

You will call your lawyer. You want him to go to court and get your visitation back.

Your lawyer will advise you against this.

In court, your wife may claim you came late, appeared agitated, and she was afraid you'd harm the kids. It'll be your word against hers that she interfered with your visitation. Unless you want your children to testify.

There are two ways you can have your children testify. They can be sworn in as witnesses in open court, or the judge can talk to them informally in his chambers in the presence of both lawyers. Either way, it'll be a traumatic experience for them. In advance of the hearing, they'll be subtly prepped by your wife, they'll be brought to the courthouse by her, and she'll have the last word in their ears. They'll know that whatever they say to the judge will hurt either you or your wife. They will also know which of you can hurt them back more if they say the wrong thing.

If you choose not to have your children testify, you'll have to give the court other evidence. What other evidence can you muster?

You will protest that it's obvious what's happening here. You're not getting your court-approved visitation. When you come for the kids, your wife is supposed to have them ready for you, but she doesn't. What more evidence does there have to be? Why won't the judge just enforce his own order?

Your lawyer will agree that, as a matter of law, you are absolutely right. But in these kinds of cases, what goes on behind the law also matters. Your wife has not simply deprived you of your children. She has allowed them to do the kinds of things that courts think are very important for children, like playing with their peers, or participating in organized activities, or watching videos under the vigilant eye of their mother. The court doesn't want your visitation to interfere with the children's normal, wholesome activities. So even if the court suspects that your wife may have overreacted—or even overreached—it won't necessarily think that your children have been harmed so as to justify sanctioning her.

You will feel your anger rising. What about you? Don't you count at all? You're their father! Isn't it important for them to be with you, too?

Your lawyer will remind you that the only thing the court will consider is the "best interest of the child." So, in fact, you and your needs and your feelings don't mean much. The children's time with you is important, but only in relation to the other important demands they have on their time.

Your growing sense of helplessness won't fully squelch your rage. Isn't there any way to fight this?

Your lawyer will show you why you shouldn't. Let's say that you fight, even that you win. It's certainly a possibility. What will the court do? It will hold your wife in contempt of court for violating its order. Then, it will threaten to put her in jail unless she stops interfering with your visitation.

But the court doesn't really want to put your wife in jail: that'll just scare the wits out of the kids. And what will the court do with them while she's behind bars? It doesn't want to fine her either: what court wants to take money away from the children's custodian? In fact, the court may be more than mildly annoyed that you put it into such a predicament.

In the meantime, your wife will tearfully tell the court that she only had the best interest of her children at heart, and she will nobly agree to make up your lost visitation and do whatever else the court asks. So the court will gratefully allow her to "purge" the contempt it found she committed, and it won't impose any punishment on her.

You may think you came out of court a big winner, but you may actually have set yourself up for a big loss later. Remember, what you really want is a meaningful relationship with your kids after your divorce. You'll be fighting soon for custody, or more probably for joint custody. In order to get joint custody, the law says you have to demonstrate that you and your wife are able to cooperate with each other and encourage each other's continuing involvement in the care of the children. If you go running to court now, complaining that your wife is not cooperating with you, the court will have a harder time granting you joint custody later—even though the lack of cooperation is entirely her fault. The court may still think she's the better parent overall. Remember, she's the mother. So the court will grant her sole custody and give you visitation every other weekend. But if you grin and bear it now, you strengthen your position for later. Your accommodation of the children's needs, as the court sees them, will be a plus for you.

Unfortunately, there's a big fly in this ointment. If we don't either settle the case or get to trial pretty soon, the court may not want to upset what has become the children's settled and stable routine: a lot of time with your wife, but hardly any time with you. So, even if you show cooperation to the court, and even if the court thinks you're a pretty good dad after all, it'll award permanent sole custody to her—all in the "best interest" of the children.

You will ask the familiar question: Isn't there anything we can do?

Your lawyer will tell you that he has considered asking the court to appoint a "guardian *ad litem*," a special attorney for the children. The guardian's job would be to investigate the children's living conditions and provide the court an independent recommendation about their custody. The appearance of a guardian in the case may caution your wife not to toy with your visitation.

But you will probably be ordered to pay most of the guardian's fees. And besides being a big added expense, a guardian is also a big added risk. The guardian may not care about you, your needs, or your feelings any more than the court. So if your wife can convince the guardian that the children are not going to pieces in her custody, the guardian may well recommend that she continue to have custody, even if your visitation continues to be a mess. It's only the "best interest of the child" that counts.

For now, the best you can do is bring along a friend when you go to pick up the kids. Your friend can be a witness if your wife doesn't have the kids ready. If she keeps up the interference, we can build a case from there.

But in the end, remember: the visitation you have now is only temporary. Unless your wife totally torpedoes it, you're better off saving your money for the trial, for the real thing.

We're both going to need it.

Your children will proudly tell you that they know whose pick-up is parked in front of the house. John lets them play on the back of his pick-up. John comes on Saturdays to cut the grass and help Mommy plant a new garden. Sometimes John comes during the week just to help Mommy around the house. Sometimes John works late and stays overnight, like last night.

Sometimes John and Mommy go out together to buy things for the house. Your children don't mind being left alone in the house; John rents a video for them to watch.

You will nonchalantly ask them where John sleeps when he stays overnight. They'll tell you that Mommy told them not to tell you about John because she wants the new garden to be a surprise for you.

The sign on the church says there is a party for the children in the neighborhood. The children will want you to stop the car and take them to the party. They haven't been to the church in a while. Not since you went away.

When you lived in the house, it was you who took the children to church. Your wife slept late on Sunday mornings, and weekends were your time with the kids, anyway. So you'd make them breakfast, take them to church, and bring them back with a big pizza for a family lunch.

You will ask your children if Mommy now makes them breakfast on Sunday mornings. They'll tell you that sometimes John takes them out for a donut and milk.

As you drive them to a new pizza place for a parting snack, your children will say you just passed Dr. Karl's house. They'll say they don't like Dr. Karl. Dr. Karl asks them a lot of questions. She asks them to draw pictures. She takes the pictures away and won't give them back. She makes them play with dolls. The dolls are naked. Your children will giggle when they tell you that Dr. Karl asks them to tell her which of the dolls looks like Daddy.

You will giggle right along with them.

You won't ask them what they answered.

* * *

Before the children get out of the car, they will tell you that Mommy isn't home yet. Mommy went to the school's Parent Association outing. She said she won't be back till late. She said they should go into the house by themselves and not stay extra with Daddy. They aren't afraid of being left alone in the house. You'll notice that John's pick-up is gone.

No one will have told you about the Parent Association outing. When you called the children's school shortly after the beginning of the semester and asked to be put on the parents' mailing list, they told you they had no record of you as a parent. Your wife hadn't put your name on the children's registration card. She called the school before the semester started and said you abused the children; she requested that you not be given any information about them.

You went to the school and argued with the principal that you had every right to see your children's report cards. You told him that the abuse charge was phony and had been dropped, and you got him to admit that your wife had never shown him any order prohibiting you from seeing the children's report cards.

The principal agreed to let you see the report cards, but he requested that you not volunteer to participate in any school function. Your wife had custody, she didn't want you getting involved with the school, and he would respect her wishes. He didn't want the school to be in the middle of a custody battle.

And he really didn't believe that nothing had happened.

The report cards showed that your children were not doing well. Their grades had fallen sharply. Their teachers noted that they had discipline problems and that they often came to school late and unprepared.

As your children get out of the car to return to their custodial residence, you will urge them again to call you whenever they were stuck with their homework. In their heads, however, they will have already crossed the threshold of the house. Their unemotional "good-bye, Daddy," will be their only answer to your request.

Your lawyer will call you with the latest developments in your case. Your wife's lawyer has subpoenaed your tax returns and served you with "interrogatories"—written questions—for you to answer. The interrogatories explore your finances and your fitness to have custody of the children.

Your wife's lawyer also wants to depose you after she has reviewed your answers to the interrogatories. She expects your deposition will take at least three hours. She said, however, that in exchange for sole title to the house, 50% of the remainder of your marital property, permanent alimony at the rate of 20% of your gross income, no more visitation beyond what you already have, and, of course, child support at the guideline rate of 25% of your gross income, plus dollar-for-dollar add-ons for day care, medical coverage, orthodonture, and miscellaneous extraordinary expenses such as summer camps and private schools, your wife might just agree to settle the case.

Your lawyer had hoped he could to negotiate a reasonable settlement without going through formal pretrial discovery. He suggested to your wife's lawyer that the custody issue be referred to impartial mediation. At mediation, you and your wife would sit down with a mediator trained in family dispute resolution and together try to work out an acceptable time-sharing arrangement for the children. Your wife's lawyer would have none of it: your wife is still possessed by the abuse business. So your lawyer has no choice now but to formally interrogate and depose your wife in return.

He will also petition the court to appoint a mental health expert of your choice to examine your wife and the children. Your wife's lawyer will probably ask the court to appoint Dr. Karl as her mental health expert. Dr. Karl will want to examine you, too.

Your lawyer could alternatively ask the court to appoint its own mental health expert, without cost to you. While this procedure might appear to be more objective and impartial, everything would depend on whom the court appoints. The court will tend to follow its expert's advice. If the expert finds against you, that's pretty much it.

So in your case, it would be better for the court to have two opposing reports, each one probably a little biased. That way the court could choose to ignore either or both. You'd still have a shot to convince the judge directly, rather than only through an expert's opinion. The downside is the cost.

And speaking of cost, your retainer has run out, and you're behind on my bills....

You will be struck by the scope of the interrogatories, the pages of pesky questions peering impertinently into your private life:

- List all persons (of the same or opposite sex) with whom you have had sexual intercourse during the past five years. Include in your answer the time(s) and place(s) of such intercourse.
- List all persons (of the same or opposite sex and exclusive of those mentioned in your response to the preceding interrogatory) the flesh of whose bodies

you have touched (other than by way of salutation, such as by shaking hands) during the past five years. Include in your answer the time(s) and place(s) of such touching.

- List all persons with whom you have discussed your wife, your marriage, or your children during the past five years. Include in your answer the time(s) and place(s) of such discussions and precise synopses thereof.

- List all personal writings and papers, such as diaries, journals, calendars, and letters that may relate to the subject matter of the preceding interrogatories. Include in your answer the precise location(s) of such writings and papers.

- List every fact that may tend to prove that you are, or are not, fit to have the sole or joint custody of your children.

- List every document that may tend to prove that you are, or are not, fit to have the sole or joint custody of your children.

- List all persons who may have any knowledge concerning your fitness, or your lack thereof, to be have the sole or joint custody of your children. Include in your answer the current address(es) and telephone number(s) of such persons.

- List all medical and mental health practitioners (including practitioners of alternative forms of health care such as faith healers and card readers) you have consulted during the past five years. Include in your answer the current address(es) and telephone number(s) of such professionals.

- List all pharmacies that filled your medical prescriptions during the past five years. Include in your answer the current address(es) and telephone number(s) of such pharmacies.

- List all controlled substances (i.e., "drugs," such as cocaine, heroin, and marijuana) that you have used during the past five years. Include in your answer the date(s) and place(s) of such use.

- List all sources of wage income you have had during the past five years. Include in your answer the name and address of each employer, your position with each, your length of employment with each, your rate of pay with each, and your yearly before-tax and after-tax income with each.

- List all sources of non-wage income or revenue (including, but not limited to, non-wage business or professional income, capital gains, rents, royalties, barter and other in-kind exchanges, trust income, dividends, interest, gratuities, gifts, pensions, inheritances, insurance proceeds, judgments, and workman's compensation) as well as lottery, gambling, or other wagering winnings (and loses) you have had during the past five years. Include in your answer the date(s) and amount(s) for each source.

- List all personal checks you have written during the past five years. Include in your answer the drawee bank, the date, payee, amount, and purpose of each check. (You may satisfactorily answer this interrogatory by supplying a legible photocopy of each such check—unaltered, front and rear—or a legible photocopy of the unaltered, original check register pertaining to each such check.)

- List all credit card, debit card, and charge card transactions you executed during the past five years. Include in your answer the card issuer, date, payee, and purpose of each transaction. (You may satisfactorily answer this interrogatory by supplying a legible photocopy of the unaltered, original monthly statement pertaining to each such transaction.)

- List the location of each safe deposit box held by you directly or indirectly or that you otherwise had use of during the past five years. Include in your answer the name(s) in which the box was held, the name, address and telephone number of the bank or other institution where the box was located, and the nature and contents of the box (indicating dates of placement and removal).

- List and describe on the attached Property Disclosure Form all property owned by you. For all such property claimed by you to be non-marital, complete the detailed Non-Marital Property Tracing Schedule attached to said form.

- In accordance with state law, you have an affirmative duty to timely supplement any answer hereto whenever new or additional information becomes known to you.

Your lawyer will tell you that you have to respond to most of interrogatories. You can rightly object to some questions, but you might end up in a special court hearing to determine whether your objections are legally valid. And, of course, court hearings will mean additional costs to you.

You will find it incredible that you must expose the most intimate details of your life to public scrutiny just to remain a parent to your children. And isn't there the Fifth Amendment to the Constitution of the United States which is supposed to protect you from having to give information against yourself in a trial?

Your lawyer will explain that discovery procedures such as interrogatories are among the great innovations of American law. They are designed to prevent trial by surprise and ambush. Before the trial starts, both parties have a right to dig for—and get—all relevant information about the case. The law reckons that if the parties see all the facts ahead of trial, they may decide to settle and save themselves the hardship of a court battle. And if they decide to go on to trial anyway, at least the trial will be conducted as openly and truthfully as possible.

In the context of discovery, "relevant information" has a very broad meaning. It can mean information that itself may not be admissible at trial but might conceivably lead to other evidence that is admissible. So, for example, if it turns out that you had sex with other women during your marriage, that may not be relevant because your wife has filed for a no-fault divorce, and she isn't claiming alternate grounds of adultery. But her attorney could argue that if you have had extra-marital sex or even if you just dated other women, then you undoubtedly spent some money on them, too. She could then claim that, by spending money on other women when your marriage was in the process of breaking down, you dissipated martial property on non-family matters and you should be held accountable for that. The irrelevant facts of your having sex or socializing thus lead to the relevant facts of your dissipating marital property.

Of course, you could argue back that if your wife's attorney is looking for instances of dissipation, she should phrase her interrogatories more narrowly rather than fish for sensational information that she doesn't really need other than to frazzle and embarrass you. But that could get to be an expensive argument. And then, the court may find that—given the policy of encouraging as much information as possible to come to light before trial—the questions, as phrased, are relevant enough.

But here's the rub. If we were to ask your wife the same kinds of questions, and she objects, her objection may carry more weight than yours. If she had sex or socialized with other men, it is likely that the men spent money on her rather than the other way around. So you couldn't pin the dissipation rationale on her. You couldn't even argue that the money that the men spent on her was income earned during the marriage and thus marital property in which you should share. That's because, unless your wife explicitly charged them to go out with her, a court would undoubtedly rule that the money was in the nature of a gift to her—not earned income, and, therefore, not marital property. You could only argue that her sleeping around diminished her moral fitness to be a custodian of your children, but courts don't much buy this kind of thinking anymore.

As to the questions about your medical history: normally, you'd be able to keep your medical records and your conversations with your doctors confidential. But, in a custody case, you put your physical fitness as a parent at issue, so the law removes your privilege of confidentiality. If your wife's lawyer can convince the court that the medical information she is seeking is not unreasonably related to the issue of your physical fitness as a custodian, she'll be able to get it.

You are on stronger ground about your psychological history. Paradoxically, even though you also put your mental fitness as a parent at issue in a custody case, that's not enough for the law to remove your privilege of confidentiality. The law does not want to discourage people from confiding in their therapists, so it affords a higher protection to psychological confidences than to medical confidences. But if ever you testify about your mental fitness, you will be deemed to have waived your privilege, and your wife's attorney will get an opportunity to convince the court that she should see your mental health records.

As to taking the Fifth, it's not a good idea. The Fifth Amendment was to designed to protect you when you are accused of a crime. You can't be expected to testify against or incriminate yourself. But in a divorce case, when you are seeking some kind of advantage, you will not be allowed to claim that you are fit to have custody and then hide behind the Fifth when you are asked to prove it. If you try to get away with that, the court can hold it against you.

It used to be, under the common law, that husbands and wives were absolutely prohibited from testifying for or against each other. The law protected your marital relationship as privileged and confidential. It considered the sanctity of your marriage and your "domestic tranquility" to be more important than the court's need for tattle at trial. That privilege has been whittled down, especially in divorce cases. Your conversations with your therapist may have greater protection than your conversations with your wife.

If you think the interrogatories are bad, wait till the deposition. You're going to have to answer face-to-face questions. Of course, you can be obstinate and simply refuse to answer anything. But, in return, the court can strike your petition for custody altogether. It won't let you claim that you are a fit custodian and then let you refuse to divulge facts that might prove that you are not. That's the trade-off you're up against.

You will tell your lawyer that you don't blame him for getting it all wrong, that the trade-off you're up against is losing your dignity or losing your kids.

At your deposition, your wife's lawyer will take every opportunity to rattle you. She will ask you the names of your children's teachers, and you won't know them all. She will ask you the names of your children's favorite foods, and you won't know them all. She will ask you the names of your children's friends, and you won't know them all. She will ask, "You don't really care who they are, do you?" Your lawyer will nicely object to the form of the question because you can't know whether to answer the "you don't" or the "do you," and if it's the "you don't," then neither a "yes" nor a "no" will reveal whether you do or you don't.

There will be no judge at the deposition, only a court reporter who puts you under oath and takes it all down. So the lawyers will furiously fight out their differences and run up the bill.

Your lawyer will prepare you to expect a hard time. He will brief you about the kinds of questions to expect. But he will miss those about your children's teachers, foods and friends. So when your wife's lawyer asks you these same questions again at trial and you give all the right answers there, she will be able to show that you first learned them after the deposition. From this the judge will clearly see that you're a very bad parent, and you don't deserve to have custody of your children.

You will find out at work that your wife has been on the horn again. She's phoned your buddies and told them that she wants to save you from a terrible fall. She's told them that you refuse to acknowledge you have no chance of getting custody of the children after the way you mistreated them. She's worried that your putting them through a trial will harm them irreparably; the way things are going, they may never want to speak to you again. She wants your buddies to convince you to stop the insanity before it's too late.

Your buddies aren't stupid. But she sounds so sincere. And you sound so shrill.

Mommy says that soon we won't have to see you any more if we don't want to, your children will tell you one Sunday.

Mommy says she doesn't ever want you to give us baths ever again!

Your heart will start pounding.

Why doesn't she want that?

Because you touch us in our privates.

Privates? Where did you learn such a big word?

Aw, come on Daddy, they will tease you. You know what privates are!

What are they?

They are boys' things and girls' things. And Mommy says you shouldn't touch us there when you give us baths!

What else does Mommy say?

Mommy says you shouldn't let us see your privates.

When did you see my privates?

When you gave us baths.

How did you see them?

Because!

What did they look like?

They looked like the privates that Dr. Karl showed us. Did you let Dr. Karl see your privates too?

* * *

It's called a plethysmograph, your lawyer will tell you. Dr. Karl wants to give you a plethysmograph.

Your lawyer will tell you that, as he had predicted, your wife's lawyer petitioned the court to appoint Dr. Karl as your wife's mental health expert. The court granted Dr. Karl the right to examine you. She wants to give you this little test. It's become all the rage in sex abuse diagnosis. It's just begun to make its way into custody battles.

Actually, you may find the plethysmograph to be the most pleasurable part of your case. Dr. Karl will place a electronic sheath over your penis. She will then show you pornographic movies. The plethysmograph will measure your arousal. Dr. Karl will then show you porno movies involving children. The plethysmograph will again measure your arousal. If your arousal the second time is greater than the first, you will be deemed to have a tendency to commit child sexual abuse.

Now that I've got you speechless, I want you to know that this test may also arouse your legal prospects. In the first place, you may pass it. Then, if your wife's lawyer conveniently neglects to introduce it as evidence, we'll do the honors ourselves. On the other hand, if it shows that you do like to play with kids, we'll oppose her attempt to introduce it.

And we'll have a good chance of succeeding. Some courts have flat-out refused to admit plethysmographic evidence because there has been no satisfactory showing that it is a reliable means of diagnosing sexual deviancy.

Of course, the court may also not admit it even if you pass. But our mere attempt to get it in will tell the court that we have information—generated by your wife's lawyer, of all people—that supports you.

Your wife's lawyer has gone a little too far on this one. She has exposed her theory of the case: throw enough mud and hope some of it sticks.

You will remind your lawyer that your wife's lawyer has exposed her theory of the case by getting Dr. Karl to make you expose your theory of the case.

Your lawyer will tell you that now it's your turn. Now you get to depose them. Now you get to test them. The court has allowed the appointment of Dr. Robert Young as your mental health expert. Dr. Young is a professor of psychology as well as a practicing clinical psychologist. He will examine you, your wife, and your children. Together and separately. On several occasions. He will also administer personalty tests to you and your wife.

Your lawyer will also tell you that he has arranged for depositions. He will depose your wife. He will depose John. He will subpoena Dr. Karl's records for review by Dr. Young.

He will need another $5,000.

He will bill you separately for Dr. Young.

You will be apprehensive about your wife's deposition. You have not seen her in a while. Despite all she has put you through, you still have feelings for her. You suspect she still likes you a little, too. Maybe she'll call the whole thing off. Maybe you can still be friends and settle everything amicably.

She will not even glance at you as she enters your lawyer's conference room. She will be, at once, more angry and more composed than you remember her.

Your lawyer will have briefed you about his style of deposition-taking. He doesn't try to score debating points. He tries to make his deponents feel unthreatened and comfortable. He tries to get them to ramble on as much as possible. The more natural their statements, the happier he is. Everything they say at deposition commits them to their words. Usually they will say something they cannot support at trial.

Your wife will tell of her growing disillusion with her marriage, of her disappointment with you as a husband and lover: how she felt emotionally unattended and neglected by you; how you made her feel she didn't take care of you right; how you always criticized her housekeeping and secretly resented her going to work; how you would withdraw into yourself and pout when you didn't get what you wanted.

She will tell how she joined a local women's group; how she learned there that the passive-aggressive behavior by which you sought to control her was actually a form of emotional abuse; how she learned that she didn't have to take it anymore; how the group provided her with its lawyer referral list; how the group also encouraged her to have an affair with John; how John makes her feel beautiful and loved in ways you never did; how the group validated to her that it's better to be divorced and happy than married and unhappy; how it's better for the children to have their mother happy and divorced than unhappy and married.

She'll tell how the children also became unhappy; how she had attended Dr. Karl's lecture to the group about detecting signs of abuse in young children; how she took the children to Dr. Karl for an evaluation; how Dr. Karl confirmed her worst suspicions; how she can never forgive you for abusing the children.

She'll also tell how, for all your shortcomings as a husband, you always seemed to be a good father; how you always seemed to love the kids; how the kids even seemed to love you; how Dr. Karl explained to her that men who can't cope with assertive wives turn to their children for surrogate sexual satisfaction: how all your attention to the children was just a way of getting your jollies without having to give any yourself.

How you will get custody of her children over her dead body.

Your doctor will be reassuring. The blood tests were normal, and there was no blood in your stool. The pain, the alternating diarrhea and constipation could have many causes.

Your doctor will want to rule out the worst. He will order a full gastrointestinal workup, including a colonoscopy, a tube inserted up your rectum through which your doctor can detect abnormalities, in real time.

As for the headaches, there are also several possible diagnoses. To rule out the worst, you will need an MRI scan of the brain. For this, they will stick your head into a magnetic tube.

Head into tube, tube into rectum. Medicine, you will reflect, is just like the law.

Worse than the pain will be the worry about the pain. You will worry about it so much that you will forget you are worrying about a divorce.

Your doctor will tell you that the tests were negative and there is nothing physically wrong with you. He will tell you to see a shrink.

Dr. Young will be thorough. He will spend many hours with you and the kids. He will note how you get along together. He will talk to you and the kids, separately and together. He will spend many hours with your wife and the kids. He will note how they get along together. He will talk to your wife and to John. He will talk to your children's teachers and coaches.

He will put you through psychological tests: the Minnesota Multiphasic Personality Inventory, the Thematic Apperception Test, the Rorschach.

He will prepare a detailed written evaluation.

His fee will be $5,000, up front.

You will not be able to take the day off work to attend the deposition of John. Your boss had a little chat with you. Your work has fallen off sharply. He knows about your marital problems and he sympathizes, but he has a business to run and a payroll to meet and everybody has to pull his own oar. You can be replaced by a trainee, for all the business you've generated lately. Your bonus is under review. And the bookkeeper tells him it's an added pain each month to calculate and cut a separate check to pay your wife's temporary child support which the court ordered withheld from your commissions. If you can't limit your divorce to after hours, you'll soon be going through another separation.

Your lawyer will report that John's deposition was quite revealing. John is divorced, from out of state. He came here to find better-paying work because he couldn't keep up with his child support payments back home. He says that your wife first hired him to do landscaping. Now, in exchange for doing odd jobs around the house and cleaning up after your wife and kids, he gets to sleep on the couch and to forage in the fridge. With a straight face, he admitted he even does the windows. He also admitted to occasional intercourse with your wife in her bedroom. The truth is he's moved in with her. But to prevent your wife from blowing a shot at alimony, because she may be having what the law calls "a resident, continuing conjugal relationship" with him, your wife's lawyer has undoubtedly told him to talk about all the odd jobs he does so he can pose as a live-in employee. For all intents and purposes, the bed-and-board he gets for servicing your wife keeps him afloat.

You should feel proud that the hard-earned temporary child support payments you make to your wife are helping this diligent young man support his children.

You will pay Dr. Young's fee, and he will deliver his report to your lawyer. Your lawyer will tell you that the report shows you are nuts: you married a woman who is hysterical and paranoid and has a lot of unresolved anger.

Otherwise, you're in great shape, except for a touch of introversion. It appears your wife agreed to marry you because she subconsciously sensed you would be too limp ever to leave her first.

As for the abuse, Dr. Young is satisfied there was none, and he will so testify. He is also satisfied that Dr. Karl is a quack and that the "anatomically correct" dolls she exposed to your children are scientifically unreliable.

So are the results of her penile plethysmograph. You registered a slight elevation when you were shown "deviant" material, but the elevation is not statistically significant—that is, the margin of error in the test is greater than the size of your elevation. You are that limp.

But your case is still an uphill battle. Most of these psychological tests were not designed to determine who is the better parent. And there is no generally accepted proof that any psychological test can determine who is the better parent. On the basis of the tests, plus his interviews and general professional judgment, Dr. Young believes that you are the better parent, and he will so testify. But all he can really say is that you're not a wacko, you have the kinds of personality traits that meet your kids needs, you put their needs first more often than your wife does, and you don't have bad breath.

The problem is your wife just doesn't come off bad enough. She's got a short fuse and she's on the warpath, but she's not a candidate for the funny farm. The kids are under a lot of pressure, their grades are down, and they have to put up with their mother's boyfriend in the house, but they are functioning. They love their father, but they are living with and are attached to their mother. Their Mother.

Your wife's lawyer's strategy is now clear. She sees you're an ok father. She knows she can't prove you abused the kids. She's not going to charge you officially. She's just going to plant the suspicion that you may be an abuser. She is betting on the clincher that the court, which may be inclined to take a long shot and give a guy like you joint custody, will not do so when there is evidence, however weak, that he abused his children.

CHAPTER FIVE

YOUR CUSTODY HEARING

Your trial will be bifurcated. After determining that there are grounds for divorce—that your marriage has irretrievably broken down—the court will first hear the custody issue. Then it will proceed to the remaining matters: property, alimony, and child support.

The three days of custody testimony will pass in a blur. Your wife's lawyer will call a array of witnesses: the children's pediatrician, their teachers, and their friends' mothers. They will all testify that your wife is a wonderful parent: she takes the children for medical checkups, she goes to parent-teacher meetings, she discusses childrearing matters with the other mothers. They hardly know you.

On cross-examination, your lawyer will show that these witnesses had little opportunity to see your wife actually interact with the children. They don't know how your wife treats them at home. They hardly know you because, when you are home with your children, they are at home with theirs.

The pediatrician will acknowledge that you also took the children to see him; your wife usually took them for regular examinations, while you usually took them when they were sick. But your wife has recently taken them for a range of minor complaints—colds, headaches, weight loss—which are probably linked to stress generated by the divorce. The teachers will recall that you attended several extra-curricular school functions, such as sporting events and stage plays; they will concede that the children's grades have suffered since the separation, that the children do not complete their homework assignments anymore. The mothers will grant that your wife has admitted to them on several occasions that you are a good father; if only you weren't such a lousy husband.

Your wife's lawyer will call Dr. Karl to the stand. Dr. Karl will relate that your wife contacted her out of concern that you sexually abused the children. She will state that her examination indicated you fondled the children and exposed yourself to them when you gave them baths.

Your lawyer will object to the introduction of any evidence based on anatomically correct dolls and penile plethysmography. The judge will overrule the objection. He will agree that a jury would be barred from considering this kind of seductive and potentially prejudicial evidence. But this is a divorce; there is no jury. The judge functions as both judge and jury, and it can safely be presumed that his learned and level head will not be as easily swayed as would the heads of 12 mere mortals.

Dr. Karl will testify that young children are usually too embarrassed and traumatized to verbalize about the sexual abuse they have suffered, especially when they are abused by a close relative. Instead, they will signal they've been abused by projecting the event onto an anatomically correct doll. Your children identified the penis on one of Dr. Karl's dolls as part of what they saw when you gave them baths before they went to sleep. They told her that you played with their privates, too.

Dr. Karl will also testify that you showed an elevated plethysmograph measurement. Therefore, she could not exclude the possibility that you have a deviant sexual attraction to children, even your own. Whatever it was the children did see and experience, it would be unwholesome for them to continue to be exposed to it—to you—in the future.

On cross-examination, your lawyer will get Dr. Karl to admit that she has no special training in the use of anatomically correct dolls. During the past five years, she has experimented in her practice with different kinds of dolls and different kinds of procedures. She currently uses dolls of her own design and manufacture. She has done no large scale statistical studies to establish benchmarks for how normal children would respond to her dolls. Without such benchmarks, her determination of "deviant" responses has no basis other than her particular, subjective opinion.

Dr. Karl will also admit that she uses leading questions when she interviews children about abuse. Without leading questions, children will not focus on the unpleasant event, and they might even deny it happened. Abused children never fabricate stories about abuse, but they will typically give inconsistent details and even recant their stories. Leading questions help children concentrate on the abuse and overcome their reluctance to discuss it. It is true that leading questions such as, "Your father showed you his privates, didn't he?" and "Your father touched your privates, didn't he?" suggest the answer expected by the questioner. But children never lie, and they would never give an answer just because they know that an authoritative, overbearing, persistent adult questioner wants it.

Dr. Karl will concede that the penile plethysmograph is not a sex abuse detector. It cannot determine whether someone who scores positive on the test actually acted out in the past. She will also concede that your slightly positive score was within the margin of error of the test, and that it cannot prove statistically that you are sexually attracted to children. She will volunteer, however, that your slightly positive score cannot prove statistically that you aren't sexually attracted to children, either.

Your lawyer will object to the volunteered answer because it was unresponsive to his question, and he will ask that it be stricken from the record. The court will sustain the objection and state that it will ignore the volunteered answer which it just heard. Your lawyer will tell the court he has no further questions for Dr. Karl.

Your wife's lawyer will then request to redirect a question to Dr. Karl. She will ask Dr. Karl if your slightly positive penile plethysmograph score can prove statistically that you are not sexually attracted to children. Dr. Karl will answer no, it cannot prove that you are not sexually attracted to children.

Your wife's lawyer will call your wife as her final witness. You will wonder who this primly dressed, matronly-looking woman is. Your wife's lawyer will ask her to describe an average day caring for her children.

Your wife will tell the court that she rises at 7 AM to help the children get ready for school. She then makes the beds, tidies up the house, and goes shopping until 11 AM. She buys food several times a week to ensure its freshness. She may also buy clothing for the children. At 11 AM, she leaves for a six hour stint at a local telemarketing firm. She gets home around 5:30 PM and fixes dinner. The children leave school at 3 PM. They take the school bus home. The bus stop is a one-block walk from the house. The children have keys to the house. They take snacks from the fridge. They are under orders to do their homework until dinner. After dinner, the children do chores. They wash the dishes, sweep the floor and take out the garbage. Then they finish up their homework and watch TV until about 9 PM. Lights-out is at 10 PM.

Your wife's lawyer will ask your wife to tell the court why she should be awarded custody of her children. Your wife will say: I am their mother. I have always been their custodian. I have always been their primary caretaker. I have always been the one to look after them. They need me, now more than ever. I love them, and they love me. We are a family.

Your wife's lawyer will ask your wife why she opposes sharing custody of the children with you.

Your wife will say that, throughout the marriage, you disagreed with how she tried to raise her children. You took them to a church she didn't like. You took them to the doctor when they had the slightest sniffle. You took them for second opinions because you didn't like the doctor she chose for them. You objected to her method of discipline. You still do. She is stern and swift but consistent. She sets rules, shows her displeasure when her rules are broken, deprives the children of their favorite snacks and activities, and, when all else fails, slaps them on the rear. But you think a parent should reason with young children. You wouldn't cooperate with her and show the children a united front. You never supported her authority over them, and that wasn't good for the children. Towards the end, you openly sided with the children, and you criticized her in their presence. You grew insistent and possessive with the children, and you harassed and bullied her to have your way. And now she knows that all along you secretly fantasized about the children. Your lack of cooperation in disciplining them was just another way you had of abusing her and the children. She doesn't want to deal with you anymore.

On cross-examination, your lawyer will get your wife to admit that her telemarketing job allows her, within limits, to make her own hours. She could well have arranged to start and end work earlier, to be home when the children return from school. She didn't take an earlier slot because she sometimes oversleeps in the morning, and she was afraid she'd lose her job if she racked up a lot of absences. When she oversleeps, the children take their own breakfast of cold cereal and milk. Before the separation, she hired baby-sitters to be with the children in the afternoon. Now, she can't afford baby-sitters on the crumbs of temporary child support you pay her. Before the separation, she also had a maid once a week. Now, John cleans the house and does the wash. You never helped her with any of that.

She microwaves most of her meals. They cost more than fresh meals, but unprocessed food takes time to prepare, and by the time she comes home from work, the children are hungry. She microwaves meals on Sundays, too.

She takes the children's word that they do their homework. She doesn't believe in helping children with their homework. That would be cheating.

She doesn't like your church because of the pastor's old-fashioned patriarchal harangues. He believes that a wife should obey her husband, that society's many problems all stem from the breakdown of the family hierarchy. She feels sorry for the pastor's wife, whose phoney piety also disgusts her. You should have married the pastor's wife.

Yes, the kids love you. They love you because you always let them have their way. You weren't home for the hard part when they were babies. She was. You didn't clean up after them. She did. You didn't train them. She did. You would have tried to reason with them then, too. You would still be cleaning up after them, too.

Your lawyer will tell the court he has no further questions of the witness.

Then it will be your side's turn to call witnesses.

Your lawyer will call Dr. Young to the stand and introduce Dr. Young's report into evidence. He will ask Dr. Young to state his conclusions and his reasons for them.

Dr. Young will tell the court that, in his considered opinion, you are much better attuned to your children's needs and you have a much better understanding of their developmental dynamics than your wife. When the children are alone with you, they show naturalness, warmth, affection and respect. When they are alone with your wife, they show obedience and a lack of spontaneity. When they are with you and your wife together, they pointedly do not show you affection, a sure sign they understand that your wife would disapprove if they did. In their projective tests—the family pictures they drew and interpreted—your wife looms as the largest figure, but you are positioned closer to them than she is.

Your wife tends to value her own needs ahead of others'. You have a hard time refusing other people's demands, almost to a fault, but you exhibit a better balance of parental decisionmaking capabilities than your wife.

Ideally the children should continue to benefit from the good points of both their parents in some kind of shared custody arrangement, preferably a near even split of time: every Wednesday and Thursday and every other weekend with you, the rest of the time with your wife. Of course, you would also share the children's holiday and vacation time. If shared custody were not an option, then the children would thrive better in your custody than in hers.

There isn't a shred of credible evidence that you abused your children. They don't present the symptoms of abused children: they are neither fearful nor overattached in your presence; they show no precocious sexual knowledge; they have no apparent sense of shame or guilt. They repeat their charges mechanically and seem to be goaded by all the attention they are getting. However, they are under a lot of stress due to the divorce, especially because they are confused about the abuse allegation and the inadequate contact they have with their father. They also feel disoriented and conflicted about having a father-figure in the house who is not their real father, a father-figure whom they know is living with their mother as if he were their father.

On cross-examination, your wife's lawyer will get Dr. Young to admit that the psychological tests he administered cannot ferret out who is the better parent. Most of the tests, especially the projective tests, are relatively unreliable because they can yield different results at different times. The stress of a divorce can skew how a person taking them will score. Also, psychological tests often do not validly predict how people will turn out in the future. And they cannot safely rule out that you abused your children.

Your wife's lawyer will also get Dr. Young to admit that he does not concentrate his practice in the area of sex abuse. Although he believes his knowledge and experience qualify him as an expert, he does not consider himself to be a specialist in child abuse, as Dr. Karl does.

Your lawyer will then call you to the stand.

There will be no one else to bat for you. Your lawyer decided that it would add nothing to your case to call your pastor to testify to the close emotional and spiritual relationship you have with your children. You would lose more than you would gain if he comes across with politically incorrect opinions about women.

Your lawyer also decided not to call John as an adverse witness. The law does not believe that unmarried cohabitation by a potential custodian renders her unfit for custody unless the children are adversely affected by it. John would deny that the children have seen anything unseemly. So would your wife, and that's why your lawyer didn't ask her anything on the stand about John. You have no other witnesses in the house except the children, and you've decided not to call them. But you do have Dr. Young and his report. Dr. Young reported and testified that the children know that John is living with their mother as if he were their father and that this is disorienting and conflicting for them. Your wife's lawyer chose not to cross-examine Dr. Young on this point. Your lawyer is going to highlight this in his closing argument. So the judge is going to have to deal with it anyway, and there will be no opposing testimony in the record.

All your other potential witnesses, such as your neighbors and buddies who have seen how you interact with your kids, have the same limitations that your wife's witnesses have: they don't know what went on behind closed doors. To call them now would be like inviting your wife's lawyer to use your own lawyer's cross-examination technique against your own witnesses.

So this is it.

You will feel, finally, the utter crush of the system. In the short time you are on the stand, a stranger in a black robe will form a lasting impression of you that will fix forever whether you will remain a full-fledged father to your children.

Your lawyer will ask you to tell the court about your share in caring for the children when they were younger: how you were there in the delivery room when they were born; how you were the one who got up at night to give them their bottles and change their diapers. No, you didn't reason too long with them then.

You'll tell the court how you tried to get home from work by 7 PM to be with them; how your wife made them yours, anyway, from the moment you stepped in the door; how you gave them a bath before bedtime. No, you never fondled them or exposed yourself to them then. Then or ever.

You'll also tell how you helped them with homework: how your wife never told you that was cheating; how you read to them before they went to sleep; how you spent time with them on weekends: praying at church, playing in the park, swimming in the pool, fishing along the creek—how you spent every bit as much active time with the kids as your wife did.

How you miss them.

Your lawyer will ask how you will be able to care for the children if you are awarded joint custody.

You will answer that you will continue to be available for them as before. You will spend as much time as possible with them. You live in the same school district as your wife. You will get baby-sitters to be with them when they get out of school until you get home from work. You can cook. You clean and wash. You don't need help to change a lightbulb.

Your lawyer will ask what you would do if you have to go out of town on business.

You will tell the court that, of course, you will let the children stay with your wife. If, for some reason, she didn't want them or couldn't have them then, you will call the parents of the children's friends and ask them if the children could stay with them till you got back. If that couldn't be arranged, you'd think of something. You're sure the people at your church would help you out.

Your lawyer will ask you what would happen if you and your wife disagree about how to raise the children. Who will make the final decision?

You will say that, with all due respect to the court, you don't ever want to sit in this witness box again. Unless there's a fundamental disagreement, you're going to do everything you can to compromise with her. You like your church, and so do the children, but you'd even give that up if that's what it takes to stay with your kids.

Your lawyer will ask you to tell the court why you want joint custody, why you think it's in the best interest of your children.

Your mind will race ahead of your mouth.

You married to have a family—to love, but also to bring love into the world. To create a bit of immortality so that what you get from your life and what you got from your parents and what they got from theirs can flow forward into the next generation and on and out from there. Your children are your life extended. They're a part of you, just like you're a part of them.

There would be a terrible hole in their lives if they were cut off from you, if you could see them only on weekends, if you had no say in how they were raised, if you had no hand in helping them grow up. There would be a terrible hole in you, too.

You don't want to do to your wife what you don't want her to do to you. You don't want to cut her off from the kids. For all that you both have done to each other, the children still love their mom and dad. And that's the way it ought to be.

You and she will disagree about the kids on some things, probably on lots of things. But mostly they'll be small things. It won't confuse the kids. It happens in families all the time. Parents disagree. Kids know that. They even benefit from knowing there are alternatives in life. So if you do things in your home a little differently than she does in hers, well, let the kids have the best of both. You won't tell them that Mommy is wrong. You'll tell them that there are different ways to cut the cake, that when they are with Mommy they should learn Mommy's way, and when they are with you they should learn yours. Then, when they grow up, they can decide for themselves what to do.

You're not the greatest dad in the world, but you're not the worst either. You're darn good enough. If, instead of divorcing you, your wife had suddenly died, the court wouldn't say you couldn't have custody of your kids, that you couldn't care for them, couldn't bring them up right. So now that your wife is divorcing you, why should the court say you're no longer good enough to have custody, no longer good enough to be their father? Just because she can divorce you for no fault of yours shouldn't mean she can divorce you from your children, too.

Your wife's lawyer will rise to cross-examine you.

She will get you to admit that your job requires you to travel out of town about two days a month, some months more, some months less. Your travel obligations are unpredictable. You can't always schedule them to be when the children aren't with you. Your wife has no travel obligations for her job.

She will get you to admit that you sometimes have to stay late at work. You can't guarantee there won't be nights when you get home after the baby-sitter has to leave. You can't guarantee the children won't be left alone for a while. Your wife doesn't have to stay late at work.

She will get you to admit that you and your wife bought the marital house when your wife was pregnant with your first child and that the children have lived there all their lives. They will have to share a bedroom—a small bedroom—in your apartment, but they each have their own bedrooms—large bedrooms—in their mother's house. There is no backyard for them to play in at your apartment, but there is a backyard—a big backyard—at their mother's house. They don't have friends—any friends—on the block where your apartment is, but they have friends—many friends—on the block where their mother's house is.

She will get you to admit that the children have their own bathroom at their mother's house, but they will have to share the bathroom at your apartment. With you.

After your testimony, the lawyers will make their closing arguments. You won't pay much attention. You'll be rehashing your performance on the stand, wishing you could do it over again, better. You'll wish the judge could just have come along one Sunday afternoon to see for himself what the kids really mean to you and what you mean to them.

Then you will calm down. You'll tell yourself that the judge will surely see through the maze. He'll get the picture, and he'll do the right thing.

* * *

The call will come to you at work. Your lawyer's secretary hasn't read the decision, and your lawyer is in conference. He hasn't read it yet either. He'll see you tomorrow. Tomorrow, after the longest night.

Poker-faced, your lawyer's secretary will hand you a copy of the decision. She'll tell you to read it carefully before you go in to meet with your lawyer. But you'll know you won't have to read it to know what it says.

DECISION

This matter has come before me upon Wife's Petition for Divorce. Pursuant to the Divorce Act, I have bifurcated the matter, hearing arguments relating to the custody of the parties' minor children first, and reserving the remaining issues—distribution of property, alimony and child support—pending resolution of the custody issue.

The Facts

A review of the facts, as revealed by the pleadings and the evidence, follows:

In her Petition for Divorce, Wife alleges an irretrievable breakdown of the parties' marriage. She requests sole custody of the parties' minor children in the best interest of said children. In his Response, Husband does not deny the breakdown of the parties' marriage, and it is thus deemed admitted by Husband. However, Husband does deny that an award of sole custody to Wife would be in the minor children's best interest, and he requests an award of custody to himself and Wife jointly, or in the alternative, an award of custody solely to himself.

Wife also filed a Petition under the Domestic Violence Act for an Emergency Ex-Parte Order of Protection against Husband. Specifically, Wife alleged that Husband (i) harassed her, (ii) sexually abused the minor children, and (iii) that he poses a continuing risk of violence to Wife and the minor children.

Upon examination of Wife under oath by the court, the court found Wife's averments credible and sufficient to indicate abuse by Husband, and it granted Wife's Petition for an Emergency Ex-Parte Order. Pursuant to the Emergency Order, Wife was awarded exclusive possession of the parties' marital residence and the temporary physical care and possession of the minor children. Husband was ordered by the court to stay away from the marital residence, Wife's place of employment, the minor children's school during their presence there, and from any other place where Husband might know Wife or the minor children to be present. The Emergency Ex-Parte Order was for 21 days, during which time Husband was to be served with summons and notice of hearing on whether the Emergency Ex-Parte Order should be made into a Permanent Order.

During the 21 day period of the Emergency Ex-Parte Order, Wife entered into an agreement with Husband. Pursuant to this agreement, Husband (i) vacated the marital residence, (ii) acknowledged that Wife was to have temporary legal and physical custody of the minor children, (iii) incurred the obligation to pay Wife child support by monthly wage assignment of his income at the guideline rate, and (iv) was accorded visitation with the minor children for five hours every other Sunday afternoon; and Wife moved to withdraw her allegations of abuse and to vacate the Emergency Ex-Parte Order of Protection without prejudice to her to refile her petition at some future time. This agreement was presented to the court and incorporated in an Agreed Order of the court which vacated the Emergency Ex-Parte Order of Protection. The court at no time conducted an adversarial domestic violence hearing or made a comprehensive evidentiary finding of abuse by Husband of Wife or the minor children.

The evidence in this case presents portraits of two parents who have been closely involved in the care of their children. The children's teachers testified to Wife's regular presence at parent-teacher meetings and to her concern for the children's progress at school. The children's pediatrician also testified that Wife timely brought the children to his office for their regular checkups and that she evinced a serious attitude towards the children's health.

Until the parties' separation, Husband was also involved with the children's health and education. On occasion, he brought the children to the pediatrician when they were ill, and he testified to helping them with their homework on the evenings that he came home from work early enough to do so. Husband has also spent considerable time with the children on weekends, taking them to church and to various recreational activities. Since the parties' separation, however, Husband has spent significantly less time with the children than before.

The parties each called an expert mental health witness. Dr. Frieda Karl testified that Wife brought the children to her for a consultation upon suspicion that Husband had abused them: specifically, that Husband fondled and exposed himself to them when he administered their baths. Dr. Karl examined the minor children, employing projective drawings made by the minor children as well as "anatomically correct" dolls of her design and manufacture. She also administered a penile plethysmograph to Husband, the results of which indicated a slightly positive reading within the margin of error of the test. Her conclusions were that the minor children's drawings, their response to the anatomically correct dolls, and Husband's score on the penile plethysmograph were suggestive that Husband had initiated some untoward activity with the minor children and that such activity, if continued, would constitute a serious endangerment of the minor children's health and welfare.

Wife testified that during the course of the marriage, she had been the primary caretaker of the minor children. She limited and arranged her hours of employment so that she could see the minor children off to school in the morning. She arranged for baby sitters to be with the minor children during the two hours or so between the time they returned from school and she got home from work, and she did the regular household shopping, cooking, and cleaning, aided by a maid. Other witnesses for Wife—some of the minor children's friends' mothers— confirmed that Wife was generally attentive to the needs of the minor children.

Wife also testified to the conflicts that prevailed during the marriage between Husband and her concerning the upbringing of the minor children. Husband took the children to a church which did not meet with Wife's approval. He also occasionally took the minor children, over Wife's objection, to a pediatrician other than the one whom Wife had selected. Husband differed from Wife in his attitude to discipline, Wife favoring clear rules and punishments for their violation, and Husband favoring a less structured approach. Husband and Wife also differed in their approach to assisting the minor children with schoolwork, Wife insisting that the minor children must be responsible for their homework on their own, and Husband readily responding to the minor children requests for assistance to complete their assignments. Wife further testified that she did not consider a continuation of these conflicts to be beneficial to the children.

Dr. Robert Young, clinical psychologist, testified on behalf of Husband. He prepared a detailed report summarizing the results of psychological tests which were administered under his direction to the parties and the minor children. He acknowledged that these tests cannot answer the question, "which parent would be the better custodian," of the minor children, but he asserted that they can indicate which parent appears to be better suited, in terms of his or her personality traits and behaviors, to meeting the minor children's developmental demands. He also observed and evaluated the personal interactions of the minor children with both Husband and Wife. He found no evidence that Husband actually abused the minor children. He concluded that, as between Husband and Wife, Husband possesses in greater measure the requisite amounts of parental attentiveness, patience and temperateness, and that Husband would be the preferred custodian for the minor children, although his first preference is for a joint custodial arrangement in which both Husband and Wife would share the custody of the minor children.

Husband testified that although he generally returns home from work at 7 PM, he cannot always leave work to assure his arrival at that time, and that his work also requires that he travel away from home for significant periods of time. He acknowledged that although his residence is in the same school district as Wife's, it is far from the residences of the minor children's playmates and lacks many of the amenities of Wife's residence such as a backyard and a bedroom for each of the minor children and a separate bathroom for them.

Neither party called the minor children to testify, and neither party requested the court to interview the minor children in chambers. Although pursuant to the Divorce Act, the court has discretion on its own motion to interview the minor children in chambers, the court declined to do so, it being the court's practice to respect the apparent wishes of the parties to shield the minor children from the potential stress of exposure at trial to the conflict of their parents in the matter of their custody. The court also notes that the tender ages of the minor children would render their opinions and desires as to their future custody relatively inconclusive with the court.

* * *

The Law

The Divorce Act requires that, in a child custody determination, the court must make its award based on the best interest of the child or children of the parties. The Divorce Act further requires that in arriving at a determination of the best interest of the child or children the court shall consider all relevant factors, including the following: (i) the mental and physical health of each parent; (ii) the wishes of each parent as to the custody of the child or children, and the wishes of the child as to his or her custody; (iii) the quality of the relationship of the child or children to each parent; (iv) the quality of the adjustment of the child or children to home, school and community; (v) the willingness and ability of each parent to encourage a continuing relationship between the other parent and the child; and (vi) the perpetration of domestic violence by a parent, whether directed against the child or children or against any other person. With regard to an award of joint custody, the court must further consider whether the parents are able to cooperate effectively and consistently with each other regarding the physical care of the child or children, and it must also consider the parents' respective residential circumstances. The court must not presume in advance that an award either of sole custody to one parent or of joint custody to both parents is the preferred outcome. The court must also not presume that either the father or the mother is the preferred custodian solely on the basis of his or her sex. In interpreting these statutory factors, our case law has emphasized the overriding importance of continuity and stability for children of all ages but especially for children of tender years such as the children of the parties in this case.

Ruling

Having considered the evidence and the statutory factors, the court hereby rules that sole legal and physical custody of the parties' minor children be awarded to Wife.

Without in any way seeking to minimize the valuable contribution of Husband, the court finds that Wife has been the primary caretaker of the minor children throughout the parties' marriage. Of the two parties, it was Wife who ultimately abridged and modified her workplace participation so that she could tend on a constant basis to the minor children's many needs. Wife has also been the primary liaison between the minor children and their schoolteachers.

The children are certainly still of an age to need the regular ministrations of Wife. Husband's unpredictable work schedule does not allow him personally and regularly to invest the same kind of time and effort as Wife has. Securing stability and continuity for the minor children will be best achieved by allowing them to remain in the care and custody of Wife.

Although the evidence disclosed that the minor children are sometimes home alone before Wife returns from her part-time employment, there has been no showing that this has been harmful to them. And although the evidence also disclosed that Wife has briefly cohabited in the marital home, there has been no showing that the children have been exposed to age-inappropriate explicit sexual stimuli either by Wife or by her paramour. Our case law has firmly established that non-marital cohabitation by a potential custodian is not a disqualifying factor unless such cohabitation can be shown to be directly harmful to the minor children. While Dr. Young did report and testify that the minor children are disoriented and conflicted by the presence of Wife's paramour in the home, such discomfort appears to be short-term and temporary at worst. It is part of the unavoidable adjustment the minor children will have to make as they become used to regarding their mother as a newly independent woman. It does not rise to the level of harm required by our case law to disqualify Wife from a custodial role with her children.

The court finds that an award of joint custody would not be appropriate in this case. Husband and Wife have a history of disagreement concerning the upbringing of their children. The parties disagreed about the minor children's medical care and religious training, two central concerns of parents. The evidence has indicated that such disagreements were of such magnitude so as to be at least partially responsible for the breakdown of the parties' marriage. Our case law has firmly established that joint custody is inappropriate where the record suggests that the parties seriously disagree about the upbringing of their children. Although Husband has testified that he proposes to be more accommodating to Wife's opinions in the future, there is nothing in the record to confirm that he will so completely change his behavior from past practice, and his testimony in this regard may safely be regarded as self-serving.

Furthermore, the evidence has shown that there are significant differences between the residential circumstances of the parties. The minor children currently reside in the marital home with Wife. They have many friends on the block and in the immediate neighborhood. They have their own bedrooms and they share their own separate bathroom. They have the use of a spacious back yard. The minor children have lived in the marital home all their lives. Although Husband has provided an adequate apartment for himself and the minor children, the minor children have no friends in the neighborhood, and it has few of the amenities they have been accustomed to since birth. It is certainly in the best interest of the minor children for them to continue to enjoy as much as possible the superior accommodations of the marital home and not to have to dilute such enjoyment by having to establish an alternating, joint residence with Husband.

Dr. Young reported and testified that on the basis of psychological tests he administered to the parties and the minor children, as well as on the basis of interviews he conducted with them, Husband appeared to have the better complement of personality traits to care for the minor children. Nothing, however, in Dr. Young's findings suggested that Wife would make a poor custodian. While the relative mental health of the parties is certainly a statutory factor for the court to consider, it is only one of several statutory factors which the court is bidden to weigh and balance. The superior mental health of Husband, as reported and testified to by his retained expert, must be set against the many superior attributes of Wife, which have been noted above.

Dr. Karl concluded that Husband initiated untoward activity with the minor children by fondling them while giving them their evening baths and by exposing himself to them at such times. Her conclusions rest in part upon her observations of the interactions of the minor children with "anatomically correct" dolls and upon the marginally elevated, statistically insignificant results of a penile plethysmograph which she administered to Husband. Our case law is divided on the evidentiary value, if any, of anatomically correct dolls and penile plethysmography. A close reading of our case law has led the court to conclude that the evidence adduced by Dr. Karl's testimony is insufficient to support a finding that Husband sexually abused the minor children, and the court does not indeed believe that such abuse ever occurred. The court's award herein of sole legal and physical custody to Wife is based exclusively and entirely on the remaining statutory factors set forth hereinabove.

The court further finds that Husband is entitled to the reasonable visitation that our statue preserves for the non-custodial parents of the minor children of divorce. Our case law has arrived at the consensus that, all other things being equal, reasonable visitation means visitation liberal enough so as to encourage an ongoing relationship between the non-custodial parent and the minor child. By arrangement with Wife, Husband currently enjoys temporary unsupervised visitation with the minor children for five hours every other Sunday afternoon. This arrangement, as noted above, was entered into by the parties as part of an agreement between them which resulted in the withdrawal by Wife of her allegation of sexual abuse of the minor children. Although Husband's current visitation occurs when it is unlikely that the minor children will have recourse to a bath—that is, when the risk, as Wife perceives it, of Husband sexually abusing the minor children is very low—it does indicate that Wife, to her credit, is generally willing to entertain the maintenance of a visitational relationship between Husband and the minor children, given the proper precautions. No untoward incidents during Husband's current visitation have been reported to the court. The court therefore believes that an expansion of Husband's visitation with the minor children would be appropriate.

The court orders that Husband's visitation with the minor children be expanded to the first three Sundays of every month from 9 AM to 5 PM. (During the remaining fourth and possibly fifth Sunday of every month, the children shall remain with Wife so that she, too, may enjoy an uninterrupted Sunday with the minor children.) Such visitation is to continue for 3 months from the date of this order, whereafter Husband's visitation shall be revised to conform to our established liberal standard of every other weekend from Friday afternoon at 7 PM overnight through Sunday afternoon at 5 PM. The court has also set forth, in the Appendix to this Decision, a substantial allocation to Husband of the minor children's holiday and school vacation time.

It is so ORDERED.

* * *

You did pretty well, your lawyer will tell you, as he ushers you into his office. Abuse charge quashed. More visitation. More visitation still to come. Sure, you didn't get joint custody. It was a long shot, anyway. And if you want, you can appeal.

Appeal to what, you will sneer. You've had enough. You were a loser in marriage and now you're a loser in divorce. If some jackass judge who gets to play God thinks it's just fine for kids to have a deadbeat drifter take the place of their father then let him live with that. You can't. Besides, you can't afford to appeal. You're cutting your losses. You're outta here.

Of course, all is not lost. You've learned a thing or two. For starters, you're gonna give up your apartment—you know, the one the judge said is not good enough for the kids—and then you're gonna go looking for John's ex....

Your lawyer will dryly remind you that you can't go anywhere just yet. The court must still rule on alimony and child support. And how much you have to pay your wife's attorney.

Your losses have just begun.

PART THREE

HOW DIVORCE LAW
TAKES AWAY YOUR INCOME

CHAPTER SIX

ALIMONY

After the court awards sole custody of your children to your ex, it may order you to pay her alimony. In most states, even if the divorce was her fault, even if she has ongoing sexual relations with another man, so long as she's careful not to marry or set up a household with him, she can get an ongoing share of your income.

At least for a few years. At least until she can raise her earnings to the point where they roughly match the marital standard. And, if after a few years she is not quite able to be entirely on her own, or to marry, she can return to court and ask for more time and more money. At least for a few more years. And if after that she still needs more time and more money, she can return again to court....

You, of course, are not entitled to anything more from her.

It wasn't always so.

In the days when divorce was infrequent and based on fault, a wife could not just pick up and leave the marriage. She had to prove her husband had strayed or was cruel to her. Often, however, it was she who had strayed and had a lover waiting in the wings. To get out of the marriage, she had to convince her cuckolded husband either to divorce her or to appear in court as a nominal adulterer himself and be divorced by her. He could not be expected to do so except on favorable terms. Favorable terms could have included a relinquishment by her of alimony and custody and the possibility of a tort action for "alienation of affections" or "criminal conversation" against her paramour. The law did not recognize a marital duty of support from wife to husband, so it would not order alimony from her to him. Even the poor husband of a rich wife at fault did not get alimony. He could only get what he bargained for.

Antsy husbands also had to buy themselves out of marriage. They had to bribe their wives to agree to divorce them. Conversely, a husband at fault who did not want out could nevertheless be divorced by his wife and ordered to pay her alimony. Alimony included a benefit to the children. It could be from a third to a half of a husband's income. For life.

Nevertheless, not all husbands at fault actually paid. Some had too few resources. Others offered a discounted, but immediate, lump sum property settlement which their wives accepted "in lieu" of drawn out, potentially uncertain alimony payments. Still others who could have afforded to pay refused. Of these, some felt they had been driven by their wives to stray, and it didn't make sense to them that their marital support obligation should continue after the dissolution of their marriage.

It didn't make sense because alimony was a kind of legal accident. A long time ago in England, when there was no civil court divorce, ecclesiastical courts entertained a limited action for separation known as "divorce from bed and board." Technically, this action was not intended to dissolve the marriage but rather to encourage reconciliation. The parties remained married, and so a husband, who under the common law owned or controlled virtually all of his wife's personal property and income, was ordered to continue supporting her during their separation. This made sense so long as a separated wife was not allowed by law to manage her own financial resources. But after civil court divorce became part of the legal landscape, and wives gained full control over their own property during marriage, the original rationale for alimony vanished.

It was then that courts discovered that a man, upon marriage, incurred a permanent duty to support his wife and that he should not escape his duty by a divorce for which he was at fault. By that bootstrap argument, alimony, which started as a device to maintain the support of a separated wife, was co-opted to serve as support for an absolutely divorced woman who owed no obligations to, and certainly conferred no benefits upon, her ex-husband.

The arrival of post-marital alimony also coincided with a growing shift in accepted sentiments about the nature of the family.

In earlier times, the family was regarded as a kind of domestic government, a state-in-little with its own legitimate jurisdiction. The political state was content to let the family state run its own affairs because the political state did not see itself in the business of providing family support services.

Families then were more than husband, wife, and children. They were a web of connections up and down the generations and across degrees of relationship. They included close friends and servants. Cultural and religious norms governed family ties and reinforced moral obligations of mutual support and altruism.

Church and civic charitable societies provided succor for those who slipped through the family support network. Public poor-houses and orphanages were options of last resort.

A divorced woman could take her property and return to her family of origin. She could also turn to the labor market. She was a free, single person who could contract, obtain credit—and work—in her own right. It is true that her opportunities were not nearly as extensive as a man's. But that was true for her spinster sisters also. It was not a function of her divorce.

Women's work may not have been men's work, but then, men's work was not so appealing either. Men's work was menial and menacing: the mine, the manufactory, the foundry, the ship, the shop were grisly and grimy—not gilded and glamorous. Men's work took the years off men and the bloom off women. Women's work was harsh, too: the kitchen, the kindergarten, the sweatshop, the bookkeeper's bench, the bordello. But for some women, it was not quite as harsh as marriage and childbirth, which took the years off women and the bloom off men.

These sentiments started to change in the nineteenth century, around the time that courts began to award custody of the children to the mother. With the industrial revolution in full gear, men and women came more and more to be regarded as naturally occupying entirely separate "spheres" of activity: women's place was by the hearth, in the private domestic realm, while men held sway in the marketplace, in the public, workaday world.

As courts articulated the "tender years" doctrine and the "best interest of the child" test to justify their increasingly frequent departures from paternal custody, it was not just the wife who would now have to fend unnaturally for herself in the hostile, outside world. It was the wife, bound as a mother to her children. In the meanwhile, the individuating forces of the industrial revolution had begun to weaken the cohesion of the extended family, leaving the divorced mother no acceptable place to turn but to the public dole or to the continued support of her ex-husband. Alimony in such cases, for both mother and child—and the administrators of the public dole—was indispensable. Eventually, with the demise of fault as a factor in divorce generally, alimony, in most states, was purged of its moorings in fault, also. It became awardable now to the wife—and even to the husband—who had brought about the breakdown of the marriage.

But just as alimony had become well-established, public sentiments once again shifted. The job market gradually opened up for women, who soon forsook their separate sphere for the workplace. And since the end of the Second World War, but especially since the 1960s, as the feminine mystique gave way to feminism, women steadily closed the earnings gap between themselves and men.

In response to these momentous changes, courts started to refrain from ordering a divorced husband to continue supporting his ex-wife when she could reasonably find a job and support herself. At most, they would provide very short-term—5 years or less—"rehabilitative" maintenance which was designed to encourage a divorced wife to become self-supporting as soon as possible. Divorced wives were now understood to have an affirmative duty to make a good-faith effort to become gainfully employed. Some courts went to extremes and awarded only paltry or token payments.

This new trend came to an abrupt end when a new theory that argued for more ample alimony rose to the rescue: Women who marry and become housewives divert their "human capital" away from the market economy and into the non-wage-paying family economy. Their marketable employment skills—their "career assets"—lie dormant and decline in value during marriage. When, after divorce, these women are thrust back into the workplace, they must compete at a disadvantage against everyone who remained fully employed—everyone whose career assets grew in value—while they moldered in marriage. Their ex-husbands, who benefitted during marriage from their misplaced human capital investments in the family, should now "equitably" reimburse them for their consequent loss of competitive position in the marketplace.

This theory was warmly greeted by the rapidly growing number of divorcées who were being dispatched from court with stunted alimony orders. It struck an especially strong chord with the chorus of feminist ideologues and politicians that had come to see family law as a central, controllable arena for the transfer of wealth from men to women; and it was duly amplified by the feminist refrain that traditional marriage itself is a repressive patriarchal institution designed by evil men to exploit unwary women. Here, then, was an economic argument to fit the feminist bill. The return that wives receive on their human capital during marriage is pitifully insufficient. It is purloined by their husbands. At divorce, these men must be made to repay it.

The theory did not acknowledge the non-economic benefits the wife had bargained for in marriage: freedom from the anxiety of earning a living; the run of a household; the rewards of raising children. The theory did not credit the wife with these accumulated values. Nor did it credit her with the planning, organizational, and interpersonal skills she honed as a homemaker, skills that later could be transferred to, and capitalized in, a commercial setting.

The theory also did not acknowledge the husband's investment losses in the marriage. He invested in his wife, providing her a standard of living she could not have attained on her own. He invested in his children, diverting resources to them which he will never get back. Now, his wife walks, and the court gives her the kids; then, it orders him to continue investing in them as if they were still living together as one big happy family, while simultaneously he must finance his own new household. All at once, he is left with onerous, ongoing support obligations and greatly diminished disposable income, but no ongoing happy family. He must start all over again if he still wants to live a married life. But he is crippled financially and emotionally. He is worth a lot less to a prospective marriage partner than a man who has not been through the divorce mill. The theory did not debit him with these losses.

Most ominously, the theory did not debit the husband with the lower life expectancy he faced relative to that of his wife—which was due in part, it appeared, to the greater stresses he endured as primary breadwinner for his family. The theory did not acknowledge this mortal price he paid for his "human capital."

The theory was supported by data. Feminist researchers found that the standard of living of divorced women plunged 73% while that of divorced men soared 42%. The sheer divergence of these numbers, which were so at odds with everyday experience, did not caution the researchers that perhaps there was a flaw in their study. Impetuously, they propagandized the courts and the legislatures. Unconscionably low alimony awards, they cried, were contributing catastrophically to the growing "feminization of poverty" in the country. Stiffer awards, and more child support, too, were urgently needed.

And so, paradoxically, just as women's employment and earnings were surging towards parity with men's, just as male manufacturing jobs were disappearing and middle management jobs were going increasingly to women, just in time for your divorce, alimony made a mighty comeback.

In the meantime, the great study began to attract some quiet, critical attention. The statistical sample on which it was based was small, and it was drawn from just one locale. It was composed of respondents who had gripes galore about their own divorces and who were led to believe that their participation in the study would help their cause. It was conducted by researchers who socialized with the respondents and shared their complaints. It focused only on the first year after divorce, which is often the worst. It ignored the fact that many divorced women ultimately remarry and are supported by their new husbands. It did not count property and lump sum cash transfers from husband to wife and his assumption of her debts at divorce as surrogate income to the wife. And it assumed that the wife would be responsible for all the expenses of the children, and the husband for none, even when the children were with him.

Then, someone found a mathematical error, a miscalculation. The decline in divorced women's income reported in the study did not support the study's ultimate finding of a 73% decline in their standard of living. The adjusted result turned out to be in the area of 30%, which was just about equivalent to the difference between what men and women generally were earning in the workplace. So it wasn't marriage that was causing the standard of living gap between divorced men and women. A divorced woman faced the prospect of earning less than a divorced man not because she was a divorced woman, but because she was a woman. And much as she might have wished, she couldn't blame her ex for that.

On the contrary. What emerged from the study was that marriage is the very best of all possible economic worlds for a woman. In marriage, a woman gains access to the higher income of her husband. Her standard of living soars from "-73%" to even. If anything, it is his standard of living that is threatened—it slides from "+42%" to even—because his income is now supporting both him and her. So if upon divorce she were to claim that he must reimburse her for her human capital investment loss in the marriage, he could surely claim, as an offset, his real capital marital investment loss in her.

And one more thing. According to the study, if married men could pump up their living standards by 42% just by getting divorced, and if married women could protect against a 73% decline in their living standards just by staying married, then why didn't more men and fewer women file for divorce? Why, indeed, did women want out of marriage at more than twice the rate of men?

In the long run, it didn't matter that the study was discredited. It had been given pride of place in the popular press. Copies were disseminated by feminist activists to judges and legislators. Its argument was anointed as politically correct. Its refutation appeared in obscure technical journals; the mass media generally ignored it or reported it as filler on a back page. It didn't matter that the numbers were wrong. The idea was basically right: an ex-husband is financially obligated to put his ex-wife in the supposed, superior economic condition she could have been in had she not married and then divorced him. That is the new, bottom-line rationale for modern, no-fault alimony.

It follows that the most important alimony factor for you—aside from your ability to pay—is whether your wife can go out to work full-time, or whether, because the kids are still young, she must stay home to take care of them. If she must, then you must pay.

Part of what goes into determining whether she must stay home is whether she stayed home during marriage. If she worked during marriage, then her claim that she must stay home to care for the children after divorce will seem a little coy to the court.

So, when things start going downhill, it would seem you should encourage your wife to take that job she's always wanted, the one you didn't want her to take so she could stay home and take care of the kids. Not only will she earn marital property for you; she'll establish a presence in the workplace from which it will be hard for her to argue she should withdraw.

Of course, this may not be so good for your kids. Unless she's a very rotten mother, you would still prefer that she stay home with them. On the other hand, if she wanted to work full-time during marriage, but she didn't only because you didn't want her to, she'll probably find other ways to get out of the house after divorce. She'll develop an active social life. She'll find volunteer work or a part-time job, the kind of job that doesn't quite pay enough to reduce your alimony payments. So, if you encourage her to work when you begin to sense the end is near, you won't be hurting your kids that much. And you may be saving yourself a heck of a hit in alimony, which you can then spend on your kids directly.

Another reason to encourage your wife to enter the workforce early in the breakdown of your marriage is to be able to get her employer to pay for her continuing training. That's how most employees get training. But if she is still at home when she files, she can ask in her alimony petition that you be ordered to pay for the professional training that she put aside when she married you: law school, medical school, dental school, business school. Remember, because she married you, her career assets went to pot, and now you have to make it up to her. It doesn't matter that, when she married you, she never thought about becoming a lawyer, doctor, dentist, or entrepreneur. She could have thought about it if she had wanted to.

It will be no defense that, before you married her, *you* had thought about becoming a lawyer, a doctor, a dentist, or entrepreneur, but you couldn't afford to support her and to go to school at the same time, so you stayed with your job and never went on to school. She won't have to repay you for the sacrifices you made to support her, but you will have to repay her for the sacrifices she never made by marrying you.

If, instead of staying with your job, you had gone back to school, and your wife, who was happy being a homemaker, took a job to support you while you worked toward your advanced degree, you might think a court would say that her career assets got a good workout and that could only have been good for her. In fact, it will have been great. The court will say that, by supporting you while you worked toward your sheepskin, she actually acquired an investment in it, and upon divorce, she has the right to cash in on her investment.

The court may not just figure out how much she earned to put you through school and then order you to reimburse her. In some states, it may treat your professional degree just like your other marital property. It will estimate the stream of future income the degree can produce and calculate its present value in current dollars. Then it will order you to pay a big percentage of that to your ex. Or it will make you pay out a yearly amount of its value as alimony.

The court may not adequately consider all the many non-marital endowments that went into the value of your degree: your native intelligence, your hard work and diligence, your parents' concern that you make something of yourself, their payment of your tuition, the public funds that made some or all of your schooling possible. The job your wife took to pay the bills while you studied will crowd out all those other factors from the court's mind. The fact that you could have gotten a student loan instead (and on much more reasonable terms than the court's) won't matter much either. And, of course, you won't be able to object that, had you foregone your degree to continue supporting your wife, she wouldn't be ordered to repay you for financing her life as a homemaker.

The court will not consider only your earned income when it orders alimony. It will consider your total income, including your non-marital income. It will consider your interest and dividends from non-marital property. It will consider gifts to you from relatives and friends. It will consider your passive income from trusts. It will even consider your non-marital property itself. No matter that it isn't the product of your "economic partnership" with your wife. No matter that it isn't the product of investments in your human capital. No matter that it did not come from her homemaker contribution to the family. Since it can help raise your ex's standard of living to the standard you established for her during the marriage, the court will take it from you and give it to her.

* * *

The law will allow you a modification of alimony in the event of a significant change in your circumstances. If you involuntarily lose your job and you have few assets to draw from, that's a significant change in your circumstances. You can then ask the court to modify downward the amount that you have to pay.

But you'd better hurry. The court can modify alimony only as to prospective payments, only as to amounts owed after the date of your filing for modification. Past-owed amounts will become "vested," and the court cannot modify them retroactively. Even if you are unemployed and penniless, you will still have to come up with the money.

Since this is your divorce, it will hit you just when the rest of your life is also in transition. Your kids are teenagers and can pretty much take care of themselves, but your wife is not yet able to earn enough on her own to approximate the marital standard. You've been dreaming for some time about starting your own business. If you wait much longer, your opportunity will pass. If you were still living with your wife and kids, you'd tighten your belt, and they'd scrimp along with you. Maybe your wife would go to work to make up the difference. Maybe your kids would work after school and during the summer. But now that you're divorced, they needn't sacrifice for your ambitions and dreams. They need only share them with you if you succeed.

The court may tell you that your change-of-life crisis is not a significant change in your circumstances. It's something you generated yourself. It's just too handy a happening to get you out of paying alimony. The court won't reduce your alimony obligations and compel your ex and kids to scrimp along with you just to satisfy your selfish desire for a new career. Your obligations to them must come first. The court will order you to continue paying according to the higher income you could still be earning in your old job, according to your "ability" to earn, not according to the lower income you would actually be earning in your new venture.

Of course, if you selfishly start your new venture anyway, and you succeed, do not fear that the court and your ex will continue to castigate your selfishness from the sidelines. They will not be too proud to admit they were wrong. Your ex will promptly file a motion with the court for a modification upward of alimony claiming—you guessed it—that the significantly changed circumstance of your success means you can better support her in the style you established for her during marriage. No matter that she didn't invest any of her human capital in the venture. No matter that she refused to forgo any alimony to help you out. No matter that, had you failed, the court may not have called that a change in your circumstances and modified your alimony downward. In granting her motion, the court will tell you that you can get away with being selfish once, but not twice, and that your obligation to your ex still comes first.

You were angry that your wife cheated on you during marriage, divorced you, and then forced you to finance her sexual liberation with alimony. But now you just pray she'll marry the guy. Now you know about changes in circumstances. The remarriage of your ex would be one of the most significant changes your circumstances can have. Your alimony will mercifully terminate on the remarriage your ex.

Unless you have kids, and your ex is working less than full-time in order to be at home with them. So, when your ex remarries and loses her alimony, she will know how to get it back. She'll promptly bring you back to court for an increase in child support.

You might think that just as the remarriage of your ex would be a significant change in your circumstances, so would your remarriage. You might think that, since your remarriage imposes new legal obligations of support on you, they should be considered in mitigation of your old ones. You might think that your remarriage, therefore, should result in a modification downward of alimony to your ex.

The court may think otherwise. The court may think that your remarriage is your own fault for which you have no one to blame but yourself. It will deny your motion for a modification downward. It will not permit you to palm off one obligation of support for another.

But wait, you're not out of court just yet. The court will consider your ex's counter-motion on for a modification upward. If your new wife works, or otherwise has money, your ex can argue that you'll now have access to more disposable income than before. Your ex can argue that, since you must still support her, your remarriage to a moneyed woman is a significant change in your circumstances that justifies a modification upward of your alimony. Your ex can argue that, although your remarriage is your own fault, you couldn't have done it without your new wife, and why shouldn't she be punished, too?

Your ex never does remarry, and you notice that it's been taking a long time for the children to grow up. But when at last they do, you can drag yourself back to court and file a petition to determine whether your ex is finally making the good faith effort the law expects her to make to get full-time work and become self-supporting.

You're too late. Your ex is older now. She can't be held to the same standard a younger woman would have to meet. It would be unreasonable to expect a middle-aged homemaker, with little to no work experience, suddenly to go out and find a well-paying job. The responsibility the law places on ex-wives ultimately to become self-sufficient must always be tempered by equity.

You may have thought that spending time and money on your wife after things start going bad could save your marriage. It may, rather, destroy your divorce.

The longer your marriage and the older you are when you are ordered to pay alimony, the more likely it is you will have to continue paying a significant amount. Your ex will also be on in years. The chances of her finding suitable employment are low. At the same time, the chances that her health will decline with her years is high. The court will sympathize.

She will likely get alimony for the rest of your life.

If you're really old, the court may also order you to fund an insurance trust for her. That way, if you die before she dies, the trust will pick up her alimony. The court will see to it that she gets her eternal reward just as soon as you go to yours.

When the time comes for you to retire, you cannot just stop paying or reduce your alimony. Even though you've stopped working and are no longer earning income. You'll have to go back to court to ask for a modification of your alimony order.

The court may not fully grant your request. If you have savings or other property to live off, and if your wife's equitable distribution share of your modest pension, plus social security, do not cover her expenses, the court may tell you to dip into your savings and to continue paying her something....

CHAPTER SEVEN

CHILD SUPPORT

When the court cuts you off from your kids, it will take the opportunity to tell you how important it will be for you, from now on, to be a good father to them. In fact, the court will tell you exactly how good a father you will have to be. The court knows. It has guidelines. The guidelines tell it how much income a good father like you must pay in child support.

You may think that your child support obligation should be based on your children's needs. You may think the court should craft its order with an eye toward what you and your wife historically spent on your children. The guidelines, however, are amazing. They are not based on your children's needs. They are not based on what you and your wife spent on your children during marriage. The court need only know how many children you have and how much money you make. It can then just look up in the guidelines how much child support you have to pay. The guidelines know. They were made up by experts.

* * *

It wasn't always so.

Under the common law, a father, even during marriage, was sole custodian of his children. As sole custodian, he was solely responsible for their support. But like most relationships, custody was two-sided. In return for supporting his children, a father could require their obedience and expect their affection. He was also entitled to their income, and he could trust that in his old age they would reciprocate his support, should he need it.

But when courts began taking custody away from divorced fathers and giving it to mothers, the issue of how to pay for the children's needs was thrown into sharp relief. It appeared that the mother, as newly appointed sole custodian, now had the sole support obligation also.

But instead of conceding that the ability to provide support was an inseparable part of custody, instead of rethinking their reflexive rush to mother custody, the courts simply deconstructed custody. They began to conceive of custody as a divisible bundle of rights and responsibilities. Custodial rights included the right to live with the child. Custodial responsibilities included the responsibility to support the child. When they took away the father's custodial rights, they didn't necessarily take away his custodial responsibilities. The father could no longer live with his child, but he surely could still pay for its support.

So, in a case in which the mother didn't deserve alimony—if she committed adultery—but the court ruled it was in the "best interest of the child" to be raised by its adulterous mother, a new source of funding for the child was now forthcoming. The father had to pay child support to the mother, regardless of her marital fault, because child support was for the child, not the mother, and the father's obligation to support his child remained with him even though his right to remain with the child didn't.

Nevertheless, in setting the amount of support, the courts took a pragmatic approach. They tried to assess the needs of the child and the ability of the father to pay. Each case was considered on the basis of its particular facts and circumstances. The practical parameters were: the child should not become a public charge, and the father should not be stymied from getting on with his life. Within those limits, the courts tried to find a workable balance.

Inevitably, however, some courts tilted to extremes. Cases were reported of fathers with big incomes paying little support and fathers with little income paying big support. Some judges made high awards, others made low ones, all on seemingly similar facts and circumstances. Perversely, the more experience some judges had in handling child support cases, the more variable and unpredictable their rulings became.

There were some good reasons for the courts' inconsistencies. In ordering child support, judges were influenced by background factors that the governing statutes didn't acknowledge. If a father had other children by another woman, and he was married to her and supporting them, many judges refused to steal from Peter to pay Paul. They knew they would be inviting a sure flouting of their orders if they did. If a wife were at fault, many judges felt no harm was done in awarding less child support to her as punishment; the children wouldn't starve, and she wouldn't get any alimony-in-disguise that she didn't deserve. If she had income of her own, then all the more so. It was a kind of rough justice, but it underlined the still lingering belief that divorce was bad and those who did it shouldn't expect to get away with it.

So long as divorce was rare, the diversions of divorce courts were tolerated if only for the amusement they provided. But as divorce surged in the 1960s, many people stopped laughing and started shouting. They were joined by a chorus from a completely different quarter. The 1960s also saw a spurt of illegitimate births. Unwed mothers, mostly poor, unemployed and unemployable, turned to welfare for support. Welfare turned to fathers for reimbursement.

Welfare did not take kindly to low child support awards. If the father had another family to support, he shouldn't do it at taxpayer expense. If the mother was at "fault" for sleeping around and not living with the father, the State sure wasn't, and the State wasn't going to take anything less than everything it could get back from the father for supporting his child. The State's indignation did not extend to getting reimbursement from the mother; she was deemed to be supporting the child directly by providing services in kind.

From divorced middle- and upper-class mothers, who weren't getting alimony, to Uncle Sam, who wasn't getting reimbursed for underwriting lower-class single motherhood, the cry went up that something had to be done about getting fathers to pay more child support. It was the perfect political issue, fusing the perfect victim to the perfect villain. The cry was framed to bewail all the poor little needy children who were being cheated by all those big bad deadbeat dads. Child support was a national scandal. Most fathers never paid a penny. As a result, most single mothers were poor. But the poor, poor children were the ones who suffered most.

And the cry reached the halls of Congress, and Congress heeded the call. Throughout the 1970s and 1980s, the federal government intruded itself ever more deeply into child support law and administration. Under threat of withholding federal money from states that did not comply, it forced one state after another to set up rigid bureaucratic collection processes according to strict federal formulae, and it made all states pass statutes that reduced the discretion of the courts in the setting and modification of support awards. It made the states pass the guidelines.

The guidelines were supposed to close the gap between what fathers theoretically could afford and what they were actually ordered to pay by the courts. The guidelines were supposed to bring uniformity and fairness to child support awards. Similarly situated fathers would pay the same fair percentage of their incomes to support their children.

But the devil was in the details. There were no reliable studies on how much divorced families spend on their children. So the next best thing was used: studies of how much intact families spend on their children. But there were serious problems with these studies. No one knew for sure how common goods and services, such as food, housing, and utilities are distributed among parents and children in a household. And, no one knew for sure how to account for savings: If parents save now in order to provide for their children later, should the act of saving now be considered an expense now or later?

In the absence of reliable information, simplified estimates were attempted. Total household expenses were divided by total household members—parents and children—to arrive at average expenses per person in the household. But this method, which, by simple arithmetic made the expenses of a child equal to the expenses of a parent, exaggerated the expenses of the child. Other estimators were tried. Researchers gauged how much food is consumed by families with children compared to families without children. From the difference, they extrapolated the total extra cost of children to a family. But this method, too, had flaws. It assumed the parent/child food ratio is the same for all other expenses, which did not seem to be the case. And it assumed that divorced fathers don't eat out more than married fathers, which also did not seem to be the case. Still other methods were employed. The result was a range of estimates that was very wide.

When the range was averaged, there was disappointment with the result. There wasn't enough to support the children without the custodial mother going to work. She would have to park the children somewhere while she was at work. She needed day care. Day care was a big expense. It didn't seem right she should have to pay for day care out of her child support receipts so she could go to work to supplement her child support receipts.

And another problem emerged. If the father's total legal support obligation were limited to guideline child support, the mother would have to pay for the children's medical insurance out of her child support receipts. The children could not do without medical insurance. Medical insurance was a big expense. It seemed only right that the father should pay his children's medical insurance in addition to whatever child support he was paying.

It did not matter that the studies on which the guidelines were based had already taken expenses for day care and medical insurance into account. It did not matter that these items were already figured into the guidelines. Day care and medical insurance were budget busters for the mother. So allowances were made for the courts to make day care and medical insurance add-on charges to the basic guideline amounts. It did not matter that this was double-dipping. It did not matter that day care and medical insurance were budget busters for the father, too. This was child support. In child support, the children come first.

Ignored and forgotten in this grand effort was the core socio-economic problem of child support. In an intact family, children born to parents who choose to have them enhance the parents' sense of well-being. Married parents manage to hang on to most of this well-being even after they tote up what the kids cost them. In the case of divorced parents, however, the court yanks the children away from the father, and with them the sense of well-being that they had brought him. All the father gets to keep are the costs. In retrospect, his decision to have children lowered his sense of well-being considerably.

Ignored and forgotten, too, was the fact that statistical studies of household expenditures produce only abstract, mathematical averages of the widely divergent household expenditures of the sample they survey. Even when the averages are accurate, they cannot, by definition, be identical to the expenditures of the many households which diverge from the averages. Guidelines derived from averages are a one-size-fits-all product. When applied to large numbers of families, they produce large numbers of incorrect results, by definition.

Ignored but not forgotten was the core financial problem of child support. Two people who share a household can live more cheaply than two who live apart. This effect is known as "economy of scale." When parents divorce, they lose economy of scale. With no increase in their joint income, they now have to pay for an additional household. This leaves less to spend on the children. When the guidelines were derived from studies of intact families and applied to divorced families, they were not fully adjusted to account for the loss of economy of scale. As a result, the guidelines produced child support numbers that were too high.

This was done deliberately. Someone had to bear the decrease in standard of living that resulted from the loss of economy of scale. Now, who should that be? It couldn't be the children. This is child support, and in child support the children come first: the children must be maintained at the level they would have enjoyed had their parents not messed things up and got divorced. It couldn't be the custodial parent. She lives with the children. Her loss would be their loss, too. So it was obvious the non-custodial parent should be stuck with the bulk of the bill. It did not matter that children in intact families share financial hardships with their parents. Even splitting the difference among all family members was seen primarily as defeating the purpose of the guidelines.

Ignored but not forgotten, too, was the fact that the children did spend some time with the father. The father did incur both fixed and variable expenses when his children were with him. These expenses were substantial. He had to provide an extra bedroom, extra clothes, diapers, food, toiletries, transportation, and entertainment, even when the children visited less than 20% of the time. These expenses were not fully credited to him in the guidelines.

This was done deliberately. The guidelines were intended to provide the children of divorce with a marital standard of living in the custodian's home. Just as a full adjustment for the loss of economy of scale would subvert that intention, so would a full adjustment for the expenses of the visitational parent in his home. This was child support. In child support, the children come first.

There were no more insensible variations in child support awards. All judges now did justice. They had guidelines. The guidelines knew. They were made up by experts.

The guidelines turned child support jurisprudence on its head. Before the federal mandates, state law required the courts to treat each case on its own facts and circumstances. General statistical guidelines could, at most, be advisory. They could not be the sole basis of an award. Mindless application of guidelines to child support obligations was considered reversible error, the very antithesis of the trial judge's duty to do justice in the particular case before him. But with the institution of federally mandated guidelines, the opposite became the rule. The courts were to presume that the guidelines were correct, that they produced the minimal acceptable amount in all cases. Although the court may yet vary from them, it must give very strong reasons for doing so, and it must ground those reasons in the "best interest of the child." A busy judge could feel safe when he applied the guidelines, and he could be asking for trouble when he did not.

The guidelines did raise extra funds for the feds, but less than they expected. During much of the 1970s and 1980s as the feds tried to squeeze more and more out of fathers, men's income did not keep pace with the rise in the cost of living. There never was much that could be wrung from poor, young, unmarried fathers. The best judges could do in those cases was take whatever they could get and throw some of the laggards in jail as an example to the rest. Divorced fathers, however, were different dudes. They had incomes. They had property. They knew who their kids were. They could be squeezed. And they were.

So it was that unmarried fathers, who posed the greatest challenge to child support collection, were least put off by the strict new guidelines, while divorced fathers, who had the best all-around payment records, were rewarded by having to pay even more.

As the federalization of family law proceeded apace, and the problems that provoked it proceeded apace alongside, the feds began to wonder why their fixes weren't working. The feds didn't like what they found.

The feds found that when child support advocates told them that most fathers filched on child support, they weren't quite telling the whole truth. The studies that supported this conclusion consisted of unchecked statements by mothers on how much child support they were getting. The studies didn't bother to ask fathers how much child support they were paying. When these one-sided studies were set alongside other studies that did ask fathers how much they were paying, it appeared that the mothers may have significantly underreported their receipts.

Moreover, when queried more closely, many mothers reported that they knew the fathers couldn't afford to pay. Some of the fathers were unemployed, and some were in jail. Some were dead.

Many mothers never even bothered to seek a child support order in the first place. Either they didn't want one, or the father was paying according to an informal arrangement with the mother, and she didn't want to upset the applecart by going to court and making it official.

Of the fathers who could afford to pay and were paying, many gave above and beyond what the court had ordered. Some had joint custody and were happy with the arrangement. Of the fathers who could afford to pay but weren't paying, many complained that when they used to pay, the mother didn't spend the money on the children. Many were bitter that the mother sabotaged their visitation and turned the children against them.

And when the studies were looked at from a completely different angle, another piece of the puzzle fell into place. Divorced fathers, it turned out, had trouble paying all kinds of bills, not just child support.

The child support crisis, it turned out, had little to do with big bad deadbeat dads. Most fathers, it turned out, were doing the best they could under the circumstances. And the circumstances, it turned out, were generated by the divorce system itself. The system took away their children, made them pay the person who turned their children against them, and made no effort to insure that she actually spent the money on the children. When these fathers experienced spells of unemployment or other financial pressures, they would just not treat child support as a priority.

The feds didn't like what they found. Fathers had to treat child support as a priority. Fathers had to repay the government for the welfare it provided their children. The system had to be tightened even more.

The feds found that the weakest link in the child support chain was the father's freedom to choose to write, or not to write, a check every month to the mother. Every month, the father experienced the powerful disincentives of the system. Every month, he felt the strong urge not to pay. After several months of not paying, he would accumulate a large arrearage. When he resumed payments, he had to cover the arrearage in addition to making the regular payments. This made things even harder. He would try to bargain the arrearage down, and the court was often receptive. The father appeared to beat the system by making it feel grateful to get half a loaf.

The feds moved methodically. They required the states to institute automatic wage withholding of child support. Now, every father, even before he could be tempted to miss a payment, would have his support payment scooped off the top of his paycheck and sent automatically to the mother. They also required the states to accord every due and owing child support installment the status of a final judgment. Now, no court could change a past due payment. Bankruptcy law already excluded child support and alimony from the list of debts that were dischargeable in bankruptcy. Now, no father could get out from under even the most onerous arrearage.

The transformation of child support was almost complete. From its origins as a living part of the natural custodial relationship that fathers had with their children, it became an income tax—complete with withholding—levied by the federal government on court-created, non-custodial fathers for redistribution to custodial mothers, and as a payback for government welfare. Its payment required no initiative whatsoever. The writing of the monthly support check, the last vestige of non-custodial fathers' personal responsibility for their children, was summarily shorn away by the child support tax.

The feds did one more thing. They allowed that maybe the lack of a personal relationship between non-custodial fathers and their children was a major cause of child support non-compliance. They conceded that maybe bringing the non-custodial father back into contact with his children would be a good thing for the children. So they helped the states set up special programs to do just that. The programs were designed to bring unwed fathers right into the delivery rooms where their putative children were being born. The deal was that the government would show Dad how great it felt to have his very own kid. Dad would just have to sign this little piece of paper proving that he really was the father of the kid. Of course, Dad would then become liable for child support for the next couple of decades, but just think, it was for his very own kid, and wouldn't he be proud. Little was said about his rights, or lack thereof, as a non-custodial parent. About his ongoing access, or lack thereof, to his child. About what to do when the mother leaves the hospital, returns to the new boyfriend with child support assured, and tells Dad to bug off.

As for joint custody and maybe getting Dad closer to his kids that way, the feds admitted that joint custodial fathers were great child support payers. But child custody and child support are legally distinct. They cannot be linked. Besides, child custody is a state, not a federal, issue. Sorry, there's nothing we can do about that.

The first thing you'll notice when you start paying child support is how small your paycheck is. Your stub still shows your gross earnings less withholding for federal, state and social security taxes. But it also shows withholding for child support. And the child support is about equal to all the other taxes combined.

Your household costs have changed too. Your rent is less than what your mortgage was, but you don't get a tax deduction for it, and it doesn't build you equity. You're eating out more now, so your food costs are higher. Your utility bills are lower, but now you have to pay to park your car. And then there are the costs of your children's visitation.

You clip coupons.

You buy a cook book.

You get another charge card.

When the children visit, you struggle to get them what they want. You buy them the clothes they clamor for, even though this is your ex's responsibility. Between the two homes, they do not lack. But you're in the red after paying child support.

You go back to court.

You tell the court the children are not suffering. What you spend on them when they're with you should be considered an offset to your child support.

The court rules against you. Whatever you spend on your children outside of child support is not child support. It's discretionary; its in the nature of a gift. You cannot satisfy your fixed child support obligation by making discretionary gifts to your children. You should not buy gifts for your kids until you fully pay child support to your ex.

You obey the court's ruling.

You stop buying clothes for your kids.

Your children are noticeably less eager to see you. They come less frequently to visit. When they do come, they look shabby.

They say Mommy won't buy them new clothes. Mommy doesn't have the money. She says you don't pay her enough. She says you should buy them what they need. She says you don't care about them anymore.

They believe Mommy. They believe you have enough money. In the beginning, you used to buy them clothes. You used to buy them other things, too. Now you don't. They believe you don't love them anymore.

Your time with the children has become a test. You can't pass the test. It's painful to you. It's painful to them. They discover they don't feel the pain when they skip a visit. Neither do you. What you feel is beyond pain.

Your ex remarries.

Your children stop coming altogether.

You remarry.

Your new wife is pregnant.

Out of the blue, your ex calls. She says she's going on vacation with her husband. Without the kids. You can have them for two full weeks. She abruptly hangs up. Five minutes later, your first children are ringing your doorbell.

Your first children have changed since they last visited. They're full-fledged teenagers now. They're sloppy, they're surly, they're rude. They stay out late.

They've been in trouble with the police. Your boy was ticketed while driving under the influence. Your girl was nabbed for shoplifting.

They've had problems with their stepfather. He was cold to your boy. Didn't want the whippersnapper getting in the way with your ex. He was vulgar to your girl. Made her feel she was just another female object around the house. Your ex told them not to make a big deal of it because he pays the bills and he's the best they've got right now.

They resent your new wife.

Your ex returns from vacation.

She makes you an offer.

Her husband found a new job out of state. She and her husband are moving there. She has custody, and under the law she'll be able to take the children. You always said you wanted them. She'll give you extended visitation. The children will stay with you during the school year. They can come to her for a couple of weeks during the summer. The only thing is, she keeps legal custody and she doesn't pay you child support. If you don't take the deal, she'll take the children, and you'll have to keep paying her child support.

Your new wife is a good woman. She met you right after your divorce when the children were still coming to visit. She knew you'd be financially pressed when she married you. She was willing to put up with it and to share the burden because she admired your devotion to your kids, even as they pulled away from you. She wanted some of that devotion for herself and for the kids she planned to have with you. She hasn't been too disappointed.

And now she's just fit to be tied. She's not gonna let that bitch toss you the mess she made of your kids and then expect you to pay for her share. She's not gonna let that witch throw a monkey wrench in her marriage. She's not gonna let your kids be a bad influence on the kid she's expecting. Your hotel has no vacancies.

Your ex tells your children she would have let them stay with you, but you didn't want them.

* * *

You've been looking forward to the day for over a decade. In a month the day will dawn. The day your oldest turns 18. The day he's no longer a child. The day you don't have to pay his child support anymore.

The letter you get in the mail has that familiar feel. Your ex's lawyer's name boldly threatens you from the top left corner of the envelope. You are notified to appear in court to determine your financial obligation for your oldest's higher education.

You didn't think your oldest could get in to college. His grades put him near the bottom of the class. He didn't care much for books. Didn't care much for anything. You thought the best higher education for him would be the army. They would make a man out of him if anything could. Next best thing would be to leave his mother and go out into the world and get a job.

Instead, he's been admitted to a junior college just a short commute from your ex's home. He'll be living at home with her and her husband, and he'll work part-time for pocket money. The law says you have to pay towards his tuition.

Your son will be 18 when he goes to college. He will not be a child. He will be an adult just like any other adult. He can drive. He can be drafted into the army. He can vote. He's responsible for his own taxes. If you were still married to his mother, not all the court's bailiffs could make you pay for his college education. It would be your choice. And you wouldn't have to give anyone a reason for it.

But since you aren't married to his mother any more, the law says the other facts change, too. He's an adult, but he's not out on his own yet. He needs a higher education to get a good start in life. If you were still married to his mother, you would surely do the right thing and pay what you could towards his tuition. But you're not married to his mother: she divorced you and got custody, and you haven't seen him much all these years. The law says you can't possibly have the same concern for your son that a married father has for his son. You can't possibly care enough about him to make the voluntary financial sacrifices a married father makes for his son. You won't want to give him the gift of a college education. You will have to be ordered to do so.

So why did they wait all these years to admit it? When they first took your son away and gave him to your ex, they told you it would be in his "best interest" to be with her and away from you. They told you that your visitation and your child support payments would be "reasonable," that they would keep you "liberally" involved as a good father. They knew back then it wouldn't work. They knew back then they'd come to you at the very end and say, sorry, but it just didn't work, you still need us to tell you exactly how much you have to pay to be a good father.

The law won't tell you how long you'll have to keep on paying. One day, you may have a graduate student to be proud of. And then there is your daughter's college education to look forward to.

You're scared. And you're angry.

The best years of your life, and not much to show for them: a few bucks in the bank, an investment or two, a tiny pension plan. You're going to have to find work when the company tells you your time is up. Social Security won't begin to help. And your kids, the ones you supported all those years, they're not going to be around to help, either.

You have a recurring dream. You see in your dream all the child support you paid over the years accumulating in a tax-deferred retirement account. Thirty percent of your historical income just sitting there, compounding tax-free, for when you can no longer work, for when you'll surely need it. The picture comes sharply into focus. The bottom line is double-underlined, and a tidy sum is sitting on it. Your eye flits pleasantly over the page. It strays to the top line which is also double-underlined. And your ex's name is on it.

PART FOUR

How To Change Things

CHAPTER EIGHT

HOW TO WRITE IT YOUR WAY: PRE-NUPTIAL AGREEMENTS

Your divorce was a killer. You thought the men who went through it before you probably did something to deserve it. You thought it couldn't happen here.

Now you know. Now you don't want it to happen here the next time. If there is a next time.

If there is a next time, you want an agreement ahead of time. You want an agreement about your children, your income, and your property. You don't want the law setting the rules for you. You want to set your own rules.

You can't do it.

Sure, you can get an agreement. It's called a pre-nuptial agreement. Before you marry, you and your fiancée can agree about how your property should be treated at divorce. You can agree that equitable distribution shouldn't apply. You can agree that hers is hers and yours is yours. But that's about it. Many states won't enforce a pre-nuptial agreement that waives alimony. If you're lucky and you live in a state that will allow you to limit your alimony exposure to some "reasonable" amount, so much the better. However, nowhere will a court enforce a pre-nuptial agreement about custody. And nowhere will a court cede its power to set child support.

Pre-nuptials are great if you're old, rich and have no minor children. If you're like the rest of us, pre-nuptials are better than nothing.

It used to be worse.

It used to be that the only kind of pre-nuptials the courts would enforce involved inheritance rights. Agreements that pre-determined the outcome of a divorce were considered abhorrent to the public policy of encouraging marriage and discouraging divorce. A good pre-nuptial agreement, the courts fretted, would be a goad to getting out of a bad marriage.

The courts were especially loath to allow a husband to contract his way out of his lifelong duty to support his wife. They feared the result would be rampant immorality and a line of divorcées queued up at the welfare office. They did not think women were competent to bargain for a fair deal from their beloveds.

At the core of the courts' reluctance was their sense that pre-nuptials just don't give them no respect. Over the course of centuries, the finest legal minds had fashioned an exquisite system of marriage and divorce, and here come two ingrates who say thanks but no thanks.

All this began to change with the coeval appearances of women's liberation, no-fault divorce, and equitable distribution. Women demanded equal treatment. As they showed their competence to negotiate commercial contracts, even chivalrous courts could no longer deny the corollary that they could also bargain competently for pre-nuptial contracts. And as the divorce rate rose and the marriage rate fell off, some courts mused that maybe some people would actually consider the ability to bypass equitable distribution not as an inducement to divorce, but to marry.

Even as courts have begun to enforce certain kinds of pre-nuptial agreements, they have not relinquished their tight control over them. They treat an engaged couple as being in a special, confidential relationship. The couple owes a heightened duty of fair dealing to each other. They have to make full financial disclosure to each other, or at the very least, each has to be keenly aware of the magnitude of the other's wealth. There can be no "Here honey, sign this, my lawyer says it's just a technicality," two hours before the wedding ceremony. Honey should preferably have her own lawyer, too.

The pre-nuptial agreement may not be unconscionable. Naturally, courts differ about what that means. Some consider the fairness of the agreement as of date it's signed; others look to see if, at the time of divorce, the wife comes out with much less property than equitable distribution would have given her. If she does, and especially if her husband did not fully disclose his wealth at the time the agreement was signed, the courts may not enforce it. If the couple moves to another state and they divorce there, the new state may apply its own law to their agreement, contrary to their original expectations. And if one's home state ever decides to change its mind again and find pre-nuptials contrary to public policy, they may not be worth the paper they're written on. All in all, some couples with pre-nuptials are just trading divorce litigation for contract litigation.

Thank God for small favors, but it's not enough. Even with a pre-nuptial, your big ticket items may be as completely out of your control as ever. You can't guarantee the custody of your children, and you can't limit child support to their reasonable needs and to your reasonable ability to meet them. You can't even guarantee that you'll never have to pay alimony. With the unimpaired power to take your children away and to order you to pay child support, and with the residual authority to order you to pay alimony, a court can neutralize virtually any property advantage you bargained for in your pre-nuptial.

Still and all, the pre-nuptial may be your last, best chance to tailor your divorce. If you first try to reach an agreement after you marry, all bets are off: in some states, courts flat-out refuse to recognize post-nuptials, while in others, they have no clear rule, so your post-nuptial might just as well be Post Toasties.

When you meet the next love of your life, you'll think you learned your lesson the first time. You'll think you're smarter and she's nicer. You'll think it can't happen here, again. But the odds are even greater that your second marriage will end in divorce. The odds are it doesn't pay for you to marry and have children, again.

And the odds are that you will.

CHAPTER NINE

How To Marry (Again): If You Absolutely, Positively Must

When the courts conceded that pre-nuptial agreements can serve as an incentive to marriage, they were but dimly aware of the extent of their concession. The ineluctable corollary, the inseparable obverse of their concession is that the law, as it stands, is a disincentive to marriage. Without the loophole of the pre-nuptial, without the ability to waive the law, there are many men who are reluctant to marry and unwilling to remarry.

You now know one.

You now know that when you marry you're not just getting a boss. You're getting two. You're getting the law, the State, as a silent second spouse. And since it's the law, this bigamy is legal.

You now know that the odds are even that your marriage will end in divorce, that you may spend a generation in the maw of the law, in and out of court, fending off the extortions of your ex and the depredations of the child support establishment.

You now know that the odds are considerable you'll end up as a non-custodial parent. Your ex will get custody, and you'll get not to see your children enough. You'll watch from afar as they grow up with the kinds of psycho-social problems that children who live with their fathers rarely have. You'll watch from afar, and you won't be able to do anything about it.

You now know that the law will tell you lies. It'll tell you that your wife earned half your wages by making a "homemaker contribution" to your marriage, and that she earned all your children because that's in their "best interest."

You now know that, once in a long while, the law will also tell you the truth. After alienating your children from you—in their "best interest"—it will tell you that they won't care enough to visit you, you won't care enough to pay for their college education, and you may be more encouraged to marry if you could get out from under the law. It will tell you that you'll have to pay for their college anyway, and it won't let you get out from under.

Divorce law has undermined marriage for men. The odds are it doesn't pay for you to marry and have children. But if you're like most men, you'll heed your hormones, not your head. At some point, you'll take the plunge. When you do, you won't care about the odds. You'll think you're different. You'll think you'll beat the odds.

It's better to think now while you're still rational. It's better to ask now, before the bewitching hour, what can I do to beat the odds?

First thing, ask yourself why you want to marry. If you think marriage means safe, steady, scintillating sex, and a companion to entertain you, you're in for a rude awakening. You're a man, and one woman won't always want to be there for you. Besides, your focus is on you, not her. As soon as she sees that you care for her only for you, the end is already in sight. If sex and entertainment is your standard, stay single.

If it's not sex and entertainment that you want out of marriage, what else could it be? Love and romance? Maybe, but that's an answer women give. They know better than you about those things. And they know how disappointing love and romance can be.

Then, how about a "relationship?" You want a relationship. When you say that, you really mean that you want a mutual admiration society. It sounds nice, but it's destined to be brief. There's only so much about you to admire.

The answer has to be: you want a family. Whether or not you have children, but especially if you do, you want to create with your wife something that is greater than you. As you are, you are incomplete, and your completion cannot come from you alone. You want to reach out and join with your wife and become whole. And you can't do that for yourself unless you do it for her also, unless you let her become a living, thriving part of you.

What kind of woman do you think will make you whole? Pretty face? Nice bod? Hollow head?

You can see you've got it all wrong.

When you start to think about the kind of woman who will make you a family, you'll be startled at how out-of-synch your new thoughts are with just about everything you used to think.

You used to think it's perfectly normal to have sex with any woman who'd share your bed. You didn't need marriage to have sex. In fact, a few of the women you bedded were married. They said you made them feel better about themselves.

Now you're not so sure you did anyone a favor. Now you wonder how you'd feel if some other guy made your wife feel better about herself. You wonder whether people who sleep around before marriage can just say no after marriage. And if they can't, then what are you getting yourself into? You begin to think the unthinkable. You begin to think that maybe marriage isn't just the fence that forbids you to make love to other women. It's also the path that permits you to make love to your woman.

When you start thinking about family, when you start thinking about becoming whole with your wife, you realize there is no room for outsiders, no room for superficial attractions. You can't scatter your force. You have to save it for the right person at the right time. The right person has the same idea you do. She's as smart as you and as good as you. And she's been saving it just for you.

You should only be so lucky.

But the point is you don't need perfection. You only need a mate who is your match and who is dedicated to making you whole. The odds favor the woman who has accepted no substitutes. At least not too many. And she'll be looking for someone just like her.

Don't worry. Just remember it's never too late for both of you to change.

Now that you know what kind of woman you want, you have to ask what kind of marriage you want. You have to ask: How is she going to make me whole and how am I going to make her a part of me?

If you're like most men, you want to be successful. But you know deep down that material success is an incomplete achievement. It acquires a human dimension only when you use it to provide for others, when your quest for power and mastery at work is turned to giving and caring at home.

If you're like most men, you want a nice home. And you want a wife who knows that by keeping a home for you she is making you whole.

If you're like most men, you want to be a father. And you want a wife who will make your children the center of her day and the heart of yours.

If you're like most men, you're scared out of your wits to say these things: you'll be branded a sexist, male chauvinist pig!

But the stakes are too high to cower in silence. You can heed your truest thoughts, or you can listen to the talking heads on TV and to what someone else wants you to think. If you don't hang tough with yourself, the odds against you get even worse. The unisex, high-power, two-career couple leads the pack to divorce court.

Still, you worry you'll never find a woman so out of touch with the times that all she wants out of marriage is to make you feel like a man. Just remember, it's a two-way street. You're looking for a woman who wants you to make her feel like a woman. You're looking for a woman who wants you to make her a part— the most important part—of you. You're looking for a woman who wants you to take back your rib.

There are still lots of women, even working women, like that. They're hard to find because they're also too scared to admit it. There are lots of working women who conclude: it's nice but not what I want for the rest of my life. There are lots of working women who discover they also need a home to run and children to rear and a husband to be husbanded by. They're waiting for someone just like you to come around.

So take heart. Be bold. Take the lead. You have to be a man and come right out and say it. You have nothing to lose. If she blows a fuse at what she hears, then there goes another filament that could never have lit your bulb.

If you've come this far, you've improved your odds considerably. But it can still happen here. It may not work out. You may be an insensitive oaf and not respond to her cues for affection. She may be an insecure harpy and take offense whenever you don't quite see eye to eye. You may hate your job and grow difficult to live with. She may love hers and grow frustrated caring for the kids. All these things used to be challenges for spouses to overcome. Today, they are grounds for divorce.

Because the alternative is so awful, you have to swallow the distaste and talk about the possibility of divorce even as you prepare to get married. If you can do this calmly, you probably don't need a pre-nuptial agreement. But you should get one anyway. Not because it'll make your divorce a good one—if it's that good, your wife will likely contest it. You should get one because the very process of negotiating it will tell you pretty near everything you'll want to know about the woman you're about to marry.

A good pre-nuptial should start with the premise that, unless one of you becomes physically or emotionally unfit, you shall both remain equal custodians of your children after divorce. It should go on to provide that you'll split the children's reasonable support expenses according to your respective abilities to pay them. Of course, under current law, these provisions aren't enforceable. But they will set the moral tone of your agreement, and that may shame the court into paying some attention to it.

Then, you should expressly waive equitable distribution. You should each keep your own property.

You may ask: If this results in your keeping most of the property, why should your fiancée agree?

The answer is: You have rejected the State's solution to the distribution of property after divorce. Now you are free to write your own law, together.

Ask her to think deeply about what she believes would be fair if you got divorced. First, ask her to imagine she is no longer in love with you, and she wants out.

She'll probably say her overriding concern is security, to have enough money to live comfortably. She won't think in terms of some fixed percentage of your property or income. She'd expect to have to earn at least something on her own. She just wouldn't want to be at a terrible financial disadvantage when she splits.

Then ratchet up. Ask her to imagine that you caused the breakdown of the marriage, that you were unfaithful. Ask her to imagine she hates you and never wants to see you again. Does that make a difference? Does she want more from you now than under the first scenario?

If so, you have a problem. You're marrying a vindictive woman.

But the chances are she won't change her position too much. She'll probably say she just wants to be sure you're not going to cheat her financially the way you cheated her romantically.

Now, its your turn. Imagine you want out of the marriage. It's not her fault. She's a good wife, but all the chemistry is gone, and you don't have the moral fiber to stick it out.

How would you want to provide for her after you leave? Notice: The question is not "Would you want to provide?" but "*How* would you want to provide?" Of course, you would want to. You'd probably be pretty forthcoming. You'd want to do the best you could. Not forever, but you'd see her well through the transition to being on her own.

Now ratchet up. Imagine it's all her fault. She has a real mean streak. She's a bitch, and you can't take it anymore.

You don't think you owe her anything for making your life miserable. But you'd pay up just to get out.

Ratchet up some more. Imagine, in addition, she's been cheating on you, and you catch her in the act.

Not one red cent, you say?

Do you see the double standard?

Her basic position doesn't change. She needs to know she won't be cast adrift without a lifeboat. She knows she contributed to your financial success, but she also knows that in the final analysis it was you who trudged off to work, and what's yours is yours. Marriage is a risk. Her risk was that you wouldn't make her part of you and she'd lose her investment in making you try. But at the same time—even if it's all her fault—she doesn't want to be left high and dry. That's fair. But if she shifts focus and makes vengeful demands, that's unfair.

You're different. You want to take care of her if you're the one who did the damage. You don't want to take care of her if she's the one. That's fair. For you to pay her for busting up your marriage— that's unfair. Your risk in marriage was she wouldn't make you whole and your investment in her would go for nothing. Instead of your rib, she gave you the shaft. You don't want to lose again in divorce what you've already lost in marriage.

It's around this double standard that you have to bargain.

It's not as hard as you think.

First, you don't have to set out all the alternatives. You don't have to specify that you'll pay more if it's your fault and less if it's hers. For whatever reason, you couldn't make your marriage work. Your goal, now, is to part as painlessly and costlessly—but as responsibly—as possible.

The bottom line is: You acknowledge her real dependency upon your continued support in the event you separate; you accept her requirement that she not be left without resources; you agree to ease her transition from married to divorced. In return, she accepts your requirement that she have no legal claim on your property, and she agrees that your support obligation be generally limited in time and amount. You agree to give her a little more than you'd like, and she agrees to accept a little less than she'd like.

To do it right, you should fund your divorce during marriage. To really do it right, the very day you return from your honeymoon you should set up an separate account for your wife into which you regularly deposit a small percentage of your income. She will get the proceeds upon divorce or upon reaching a certain advanced age, whichever comes first. Your pre-nuptial should provide that this account will represent your entire financial obligation to her in the event of divorce. If you fail to fund it appropriately, or you make improper withdrawals, you will owe her the difference, with interest.

You can get fancy. You can pay the tax on the account's income as it builds. That way, it will accrue tax-free to your wife. You can put the funds into escrow, trust, life insurance, or an annuity. That would remove the funds from your direct control and possibly provide some tax and estate planning advantages.

You can get even fancier. You can calibrate the percentage you pay with the level of income you earn. The higher your income, the higher the percentage you pay, just like federal income tax. If she has special concerns, such as health insurance, you can provide for them, too.

To make things really fair and square, she must agree to set up a similar account for you. That way, if she turns into an uncompromising careerist after all, you are similarly covered. Even if her earnings are marginal, her account will "equitably" offset yours.

This kind of arrangement allows you to plan rationally for an irrational event. At every moment, you will know exactly what your exposure is. You have already provided for it: a sort of divorce insurance.

The trick is to set a fair rate of funding. The parameters are: how much you can afford to set aside without sabotaging your other financial goals, and how much your ex will need at some unknown time in the future. While the odds of divorce are high, they are higher at certain times than at others. They depend on the number of years you stay married: they start out low, then they rise, and if you succeed in scratching your seven-year itch, they turn over and start to decline. They also depend on the prevailing propensity of married couples to divorce. So, an estimate of how much your ex will need at any given time is fraught with uncertainty. On the other hand, your ongoing financial needs are relatively easier to quantify than hers. All other things being equal, you will come up with a rate that is weighted more by what you think you can afford than by what she thinks she might need; it should produce an amount that will neither discourage you from marrying her nor encourage her to divorce you.

But all other things are not equal. Out there, lurking in the background, is the law. The law tells her she can get a pretty piece of your property, plus alimony. Her lawyer tells her that's the minimum she'll need. Her friends tell her that's the least she deserves. So you're not just bargaining with her. You're also bargaining with the shadow of the law, and the shadow knows.

You arrive, at last, at the moment of truth. If she insists on getting what the law will give her, you still have time to tell her she can have the law. And get the hell out.

CHAPTER TEN

How To Change Things: We're All In This Together

Divorce law has undermined marriage for men. Only half will marry well enough to elude entanglement. Only a few will divorce deftly enough to escape unscathed.

The few will have a few good lawyers. These lawyers will be skilled litigators who, from day one, are prepared to go to trial and to extend a hunk of credit to their male clients. They know that their opponents, the wives' attorneys, will often carry too many cases to litigate them competently. Rather than face a tough, well-prepared adversary and be humiliated by him, these wives' attorneys will prefer to settle, on terms less favorable than they would get at trial. They will also reckon that the parties' estate cannot afford two litigators' fees and that their time at trial against a worthy opponent will not be fully compensated anyway.

So much for the few. As for you, you're going to have to get a much earlier start. To make marriage safe for you, you're going to have to make divorce safe for all men. You're going to have to change the law.

149

To change the law, you'll need a near focus and a far focus. The near focus is the list of laws you want to change. The far focus is your political agenda to get the government out of your personal life, and keep it out.

The first law you have to change is custody. The doctrine of *parens patriae* and the "best interest of the child" standard have been fonts of single-parent family creation for over a century; they must be defanged. No court should have carte blanche to strip you of custody so long as you're not a danger to your children. Even if your ex is a better mother than you are a father, your kids still need you and you need them, now more than ever.

Instead of choosing a custodian and creating a non-custodian, the court must be charged to preserve as much as possible of the two-parent environment for the children. It must give every divorcing family two related assurances: one, to the children, that their relationship with their parents—both parents—will not be unduly upset; the other, to the parents, that they will both remain full-fledged parents, notwithstanding their divorce from each other. It follows that joint legal and physical custody, which prevailed during the parents' marriage, should be the presumptive outcome of post-divorce custody determinations in all states. The court may divorce only the parents, not the children. Within this broad rubric, a variety of flexible, shared parenting arrangements may be tailored by the court to meet the diverse and changing needs of the children. The parent who tries to derail the other's relationship with the children shall forfeit, measure-for-measure, his or her own relationship with them. If the children must lose a parent, it should be the terrorist, not the target.

The second law you have to change is child support. The disastrous development of sole maternal custody would not have been possible without the court's brute power to push the father away with one hand while pulling on his purse strings with the other. This unnatural bifurcation of custody and support by which a father is forced to finance the filching of his own children by the court must be thoroughly expunged from the law.

Only to the extent that a fit father's custodial relationship is preserved by the court may the court justly stake a claim to his income for the benefit of the mother's custodial relationship. By so doing, the court would be correctly reconstructing the father's rights and responsibilities as they prevailed during the marriage. Conversely, if the court relieves a fit father of his custodial function against his will, it must also relieve him of his support function. Of course, a fit father who rejects the court's preservation of his custodial function should not be able to reject his support function, too, unless the mother agrees and can adequately support the children on her own.

The guideline approach to setting support must also go. It is simply unjust to base child support on crude average statistical estimates that may have no relevance to a particular divorcing family. Courts must be returned to their traditional task of doing justice in individual cases.

The standard for setting child support should be the reasonable needs of the particular child balanced against the resources and reasonable needs of the parents, not what the abstract guideline number may prescribe. As much support as possible should be spent by each parent directly on the children as well as on third-party providers of services to the children before any funds are ordered transferred from one parent to the other. If fathers were to see their custodial status and function preserved by the court and their support obligation honed to what their children really require, their resistance to court confiscation of their income would vanish.

Just as fathers are held accountable for making payments, so mothers must be held accountable for the expenditure of those payments on the children. Because the State's current interest in child support is limited to assuring that the mother will not come to it for welfare, it loses all interest in the child the moment the money hits the mother's pocket. But the State owes the father a fiduciary assurance that the income it expropriates from him, purportedly for the benefit of his children, is actually spent on them and not on anybody else. Recipient accountability would go a long way towards making child support an honest deal.

The third law you have to change is alimony. The current regime makes marriage a sinecure, a risk-free deal for her, but a belly-upper for you. The only justification for alimony today is to smooth the transition from married to single, from supported to self-supporting. Real economic partnerships don't indemnify partners for lost opportunity—for what they could have made elsewhere had they not joined the failed partnership. Partners in a real economic partnership take their risks and their loses, and move on. Alimony, except for the aged or infirm, should be modest and brief.

The fourth law you have to change is equitable distribution. This Robin Hood rule underwrites your wife to divorce you.

There is historical irony here. Under the early common law, a married woman could not generate separate property; her earnings belonged to her husband. The granting of separate property rights to a wife was considered a great advance. We have now come nearly full circle. Now, a husband cannot generate separate property, either. The capitalization of a wife's homemaker contribution into an economic claim to potentially all her husband's earnings strikes a blow to marital stability because all she has to do is stake the money and run.

The fifth law you have to change is the domestic violence code. It stimulates too many false, self-serving accusations in custody battles. Litigants know that judges will bolt at the prospect of placing children in the custody of an accused abuser. When the accusation cannot be corroborated, its effect may linger on in a denial of custody to the accused.

The antidote is three-fold. First, courts must be reminded that the vast majority of divorcing parents are not abusers. Therefore, when judges yield to the exaggerated emotions of an abuse hearing, they inevitably end up punishing many innocent people: parents, by denying them custody, and children, by denying them parents. Denials of custody or joint custody to parents who are accused but not found guilty of abuse must therefore be held to strict scrutiny on appeal. The presumption on appeal must be that the trial judge may have been prejudiced by the unproven abuse charge. Second, in the context of a custody case, the law must require a higher standard of proof than a preponderance of the evidence, especially when there is the prospect that the court might issue protective orders that yank the accused away from his home and children, and result in delivering control of the custody case to the accuser. Finally, intentionally false allegations of abuse should result in a strong presumption against awarding custody to the accuser.

The sixth law you have to change is the rule allowing a court to ignore the provisions of pre-nuptial and divorce settlement agreements governing custody and child support. This rule presumes that parents, who are postured as adversaries at divorce, will routinely seek to maximize their respective post-divorce out-comes at their children's expense. This is much too cynical a view. When parents are allowed to maintain normal contact with their children after divorce, they continue to care deeply about their children's welfare, and they can be expected to be as finan-cially forthcoming and altruistic as their married counterparts. The posturing of divorcing parents as adversaries and the wrenching of fathers away from their children are themselves products of the law's meddling, so naturally the law seeks to escape responsibility by blaming the parents. The supervisory role of the court in pre-nuptial and divorce settlement agree-ments concerning custody and child support should at least be limited to ensuring "reasonable" outcomes, similar to the situation now with regard to alimony. Agreements between divorcing par-ents should as much as possible be enforced as the bona fide con-tracts they are.

At the core of all these issues are the special privileges that the law has designed for divorcing women. The gender-neutral lan-guage in which the law couches these privileges does not blunt their expected applications: in many jurisdictions, the "best inter-est of the child" is still a code-phrase for mother custody; guide-line child support is welfare for mothers; alimony is unemploy-ment insurance for ex-wives; equitable distribution is communism for middle- and upper-class women. Saving savvy women from the provisions of their pre-nuptials is the last refuge of chivalry.

To preserve these perks, especially child support, the govern-ment commands an extensive enforcement apparatus, a veritable gulag, complete with sophisticated surveillance and compliance capabilities such as computer-based tracing, license revocation, asset confiscation, and incarceration. The face of this regime is decidedly Orwellian.

If you're single and childless, you don't yet see the face. If you're married with children, you can glimpse it now and then around the corner as it plays hide-and-seek with your wife. Only a divorce still separates you from the gulag. You can't rest too easily because you know the odds. Besides, what is now "public policy" for divorced men may before long become *de rigueur* for married men also. You may soon hear the usual special interest groups plead that it's child abuse if you don't provide your kids with the best of everything that the State determines you can afford, and that the State's *parens patriae* interest in the welfare of children, plus the "best interest of the child" rule, give it the right—nay, the duty!—to take your children away from you and raise them properly, at your expense, of course.

There is already talk among family policy wonks of having the State issue parenting licenses. Having children without a parenting license would be an offense. Before you could get the license, you would have to take a State-sponsored parenting course. The State will teach you everything you have to know about being a parent. You will then have to pass a State parenting test. If later in real life you fail at official parenting, the State will say you should have known better because they told you so, and they will hold you accountable. Perhaps by then some cockeyed court will already have ruled that your children have the right to sue you for a college education because it would be unfair to treat the children of intact marriages any less well than the children of divorce.

To get to these laws from the ones already on the books, all you have to do is draw a straight line down the slippery slope.

So, if you're married, and even if you're still single, you have to worry about divorce. Even if you manage to beat the odds, you have to worry that the State's posture in divorce will become its model for regulating marriage, too. You may be safe now, but you're next.

So your far focus in changing the law—your political agenda—must be to reduce the power of the government over the family. It must be the far focus of all men—single, married, and divorced—because all men ultimately are at risk.

You may be wondering how it has came to this, that the natural act of man to marry and have children has come to be so fraught with danger. The answer is staring at you in the mirror.

In a democratic society, the government must rule by consent of the governed. In order for the government to do anything, it must convince you that you have a problem that it can fix best. Once it has convinced you, you will also consent to be taxed to finance its efforts. When you go sour every so often on the taxes, the government will borrow whatever it takes to make you happy and then come back to you later with the tax bill.

The government is engaged in an ongoing search for your problems so it can take your money to build the bureaucracies it needs to fix your problems. It has a natural tendency to grow big at the expense of every other element of society.

Over the last few centuries, government has roughed it up with the church, big business, and, most recently, the family. Its successes in all three areas have come from posing as a counterweight, a rescuer of the poor and defenseless from the excesses of the powerful and the entrenched. Often, it served to correct serious imbalances. Unfortunately, once in the fray, sometimes it overstays its invitation and becomes as pushy and bossy as those it displaced.

In government's struggle with the family, women and children have been its constituencies. Even before women got the vote and could directly affect the involvement of government in family life, their plaints were heard sympathetically by gallant ruling males whose instincts were offended by the excesses of their bawdier brethren. The few drunken louts who got custody of their children under the common law were the first pretexts for taking custody away from all men.

When government peddles post-divorce custodial and financial benefits to any woman who divorces a husband not at fault, it buys her out of her marriage. The government may flatter itself that it has made her life a bit more stable, but it has in fact made every other marriage a lot more unstable. A man is in natural opposition to government intrusion into his family. He accepts the obligation to maintain his wife. He assumes the burden of supporting his children. He expects the latitude to carry out these decisions. He doesn't want the government upstaging him. If the government wants to come to the aid of those few wives and children whose husbands and fathers fail and flee, that's fine. But it's not fine for the government to take away the children of the average guy whose wife gets a no-fault divorce, and then make him pay her for the privilege. The government has gone too far.

You never had to change the law before. You want to know how to go about it.

You have to draft a bill, get it sponsored in your legislature, and lobby to get it passed.

Obviously, you can't do it alone.

You'll have to corral other men who are going through the same wringer. Odds are there will be at least one lawyer among them who can help you with drafting. Sure as shootin', you'll also find a second wife who wants to help you organize a group to help her husband. If you're lucky, there may already be a men's group in your area. Join, and convince them to back your project.

When the time comes, you'll have to troupe down to your state capital and speak face-to-face with the lawmakers. Let them know there are thousands of other men out there just like you who'll be watching their vote on your bill.

Your bill will have to clear the usual hurdles. It'll be assigned to a committee in each house of the legislature, from which it must pass out in order to merit a full floor vote. You'll have to testify in committee on behalf of your bill, and you'll have to collar as many good supporting witnesses as possible. You'll also have to muster your supporters to call and write every committee member in advance of the vote. It'll be a full time job, and more.

In short order, you'll meet the opposition. The feminists who spout equality only when it gets them an advantage will fight to keep their lopsided advantages in property, custody, and support. They'll complain that joint custody will result in less support for women, and they'll accuse fathers of wanting it only to get out of paying child support. Some hidebound bar associations will say joint custody doesn't work because they fear it will serve as a model for non-adversarial divorce. They'll jealously shield the system from any streamlining that cuts them out of the picture. Some refractory judges will oppose joint custody because they still revel in the role of *parens patriae* and guarantor of "stability" for mothers and children. They'll swear by the guidelines, which take all the work out of setting support. Some child support enforcement administrators will resist any move to downsize their involvement in divorce because the first rule of bureaucracy is to upsize. The media will be there, too; most will feed on the feminist hype, and any dad who can't make payments they'll dumbly dub a deadbeat.

They'll be well financed. They'll have government grants, payrolled lobbyists, and expense accounts. You'll have enough money to print up flyers and make some long distance phone calls. But don't let 'em scare you. You'll have the most compelling assets: the good people—men and women—of your group who are living proof that there is something dreadfully wrong with the system. You'll be offering a just and sober alternative. Your legislators will know in their hearts you deserve a break.

While you're busy getting your bill passed, you'll also have to stop the opposition's. They'll be trying to limit joint custody, to make child support even more draconian, and to expand the domestic violence code into a catchall for male entrapment. You'll have to go into the breach against them. If you accomplish nothing more than damming the flood of feminist family law bills, you'll have done yeoman's service.

Throughout, you'll have to let the pols know they can't run on an anti-father platform anymore. Tell the next candidate who promises to crack down on deadbeat dads how many votes he's just lost. Tell him he's lost all the divorced men, all their mothers and fathers, all their sisters and brothers, and all their second wives. Let it sink in that there are lots of women who hurt when men hurt. Write a letter to your local paper, and don't pull any punches.

You won't get all the laws you want the first time around. Maybe you won't get any. But you'll establish yourself as a credible, responsible voice on a vital issue. And you'll spook the opposition. The next time, what you say won't sound so extreme, and by then the problem will have gotten even worse. You'll pick up votes on that alone.

They say we have a government of laws, not men.

Show 'em it's of men, too.

SELECTED BIBLIOGRAPHY

The secondary literature in family law is vast and variegated, and this brief bibliography does not pretend to be either exhaustive or representative. Rather, it was selected primarily to point the reader to supportive supplemental readings on topics featured in this book.

"A Man's Place." *The New York Times Magazine*, May 16, 1999, pp. 48, 64-68, 73-74.

Abraham, Jed H. "An Interpretation of Illinois' New Joint Custody Amendments." *Illinois Bar Journal*, vol. 75 no. 6, February 1987, pp. 332-40.

Abraham, Jed H. "*The Divorce Revolution* Revisited: A Counter-Revolutionary Critique." *Northern Illinois University Law Review*, vol. 9 no. 2, 1989, pp. 251-98; *American Journal of Family Law*, vol. 3 no. 2, Summer 1989, pp. 87-144.

Abraham, Jed H. "Biased Report: A Critique of the Domestic Relations Sections of *The 1990 Report of the Illinois Task Force on Gender Bias in the Courts.*" *American Journal of Family Law*, vol. 5 no. 2, Summer 1991, pp. 93-208.

Abraham, Jed H. "Why Men Fight for Their Kids: How Bias in the System Puts Dads at a Disadvantage." *Family Advocate*, vol. 17 no.1, Summer 1994, pp. 48-52, 56.

Alimony: New Strategies for Pursuit and Defense. Chicago: Section of Family Law, American Bar Association, 1988.

Amneus, Daniel. *The Garbage Generation: The Consequences of the Destruction of the Two-Parent Family and the Need to Stabilize it by Strengthening Its Weakest Link, the Father's Role*. Alhambra, CA: Primrose Press, 1990.

Applewhite, Ashton. *Cutting Loose: Why Women Who End Their Marriages Do So Well*. New York: HarperCollins Publishers, 1997.

Atkinson, Jeff. *Modern Child Custody Practice*. Charlottesville, VA: The Michie Company, 1986 & Supps.

Atkinson, Jeff. *The American Bar Association Guide to Family Law*. New York: Times Books, 1996.

Baber, Asa. *Naked at Gender Gap: A Man's View of the War Between the Sexes*. New York: Birch Lane Press, 1992.

Baskerville, Stephen. "Why is Daddy in Jail?" *The Women's Quarterly*, no. 18, Winter 1999, pp. 21-29; *The Children's Advocate,* vol. 12 no. 10, July/August 1999, pp. 1, 21-22.

Becker, Gary S. *An Economic Analysis of the Family*. Seventeenth Geary Lecture. Dublin: The Economic and Social Research Institute, 1985.

Beller, Andrea H. & John W. Graham. *Small Change: The Economics of Child Support*. New Haven: Yale University Press, 1993.

Bender, William N. & Lynn Brannon. "Victimization of Non-Custodial Parents, Grandparents, and Children as a Function of Sole Custody: Views of the Advocacy Groups and Research Support." *Journal of Divorce and Remarriage*, vol. 21 nos. 3/4, 1994, pp. 81-114.

Bieniewicz, Donald J. "In Practice: A Fair-Shares Formula for Child Support." *Balance,* vol. 1 no. 2, Winter 1994/95, pp. 32-42.

Blankenhorn, David. *Fatherless America: Confronting Our Most Urgent Social Problem*. New York: Basic Books, 1995.

Braver, Sanford L. & Diane O'Connell. *Divorced Dads: Shattering the Myths*. New York: Jeremy P. Tarcher/Putnam, 1998.

Brinig, Margaret F. & Douglas W. Allen. *"These Boots are Made for Walking": Why Wives File for Divorce*. Paper presented to Canadian Law and Economics Association Meeting, 1998.

Canacakos, Ellen. "Joint Custody as a Fundamental Right." *Arizona Law Review,* vol. 23, 1981, pp. 785-800.

Chambers, David L. *Making Fathers Pay: The Enforcement of Child Support*. Chicago: The University of Chicago Press, 1979.

Christensen, Bryce J., ed. *The Family Wage: Work, Gender, and Children in the Modern Economy*. Rockford, IL: The Rockford Institute, 1988.

Christensen, Bryce J., ed. *The Retreat from Marriage: Causes and Consequences*. Lanham, MD: University Press of America, 1990.

Christensen, Ferrel. "Science, Government and Ideology." *Balance*, vol. 1 no. 4, Fall 1995, pp. 31-36.

Clarke, Sally C. "Advance Report of Final Divorce Statistics, 1989 and 1990." *Monthly Vital Statistics Report,* vol. 43 no. 9 Supp., March 22, 1995. Hyattsville, MD: National Center for Health Statistics, 1995.

Clawar, Stanley S. & Brynne V. Rivlin. *Children Held Hostage: Dealing with Programmed and Brainwashed Children.* Chicago: Section of Family Law, American Bar Association, 1991.

Cook, James A. "Joint Custody, Sole Custody: A New Statute Reflects a New Perspective." *Conciliation Courts Review,* vol. 18 no. 1, June 1980, pp. 31 -45; republished as "California's Joint Custody Statute," in Folberg, Jay, ed., *Joint Custody and Shared Parenting,* pp. 168-83. Washington, DC: BNA Books, 1984.

Deech, Ruth. "Divorce Law and Empirical Studies." *The Law Quarterly Review,* vol. 106, April 1990, p. 229-45.

Dobrish, Robert Z. "Representing the Father Who Is Accused of Child Sexual Abuse." *Family Law Quarterly,* vol. 23 no. 3, Fall 1989, pp. 465-475.

Doherty, Brian. "Big Daddy: Can the Feds Support Child Support?" *Reason,* June 1996, pp. 46-48.

Domestic Violence. San Diego: Greenhaven Press, Inc., 1996.

Doyle, Richard F. *The Rape of the Male.* St. Paul: Poor Richard's Press, 1976.

Duncan, Greg J. & Saul D. Hoffman. "A Reconsideration of The Economic Consequences of Marital Dissolution." *Demography,* vol. 22 no. 4, November 1985, pp. 485-97.

Eberling, Kay. "The Failure of Feminism." *Newsweek,* November 19, 1990, p.9.

Elkin, Myer. "Joint Custody: A Self-Determined Structure for Shared Parenting." *Conciliation Courts Review,* vol. 22 no. 2, December 1984, pp. v-vii.

Farrell, Warren. *The Myth of Male Power.* New York: Simon & Shuster, 1993.

Fay, Robert E. "The Disenfranchised Father." *Advanced Pediatrics,* vol. 36, 1989, pp. 407-30; *American Journal of Family Law,* vol 9, no. 1, Spring 1995, pp. 17-33.

Felton, Eric. "Divorce's Atom Bomb: Child Sex Abuse." *Insight,* November 25, 1991, pp. 6-10, 34-36.

Folberg, Jay, ed. *Joint Custody and Shared Parenting,* Washington, DC: BNA Books, 1984.

Folberg, Jay & Marva Graham. "Joint Custody of Children Following Divorce." *University of California at Davis Law Review,* vol. 12, 1979, pp. 523-81.

Furchtgott-Roth, Diana & Christine Stolba. *Women's Figures: An Illustrated Guide to the Economic Progress of Women in America.* Washington, DC/Arlington, VA: The AEI Press/Independent Women's Forum, 1999.

Gallagher, Maggie. *The Abolition of Marriage: How We Destroy Lasting Love.* Washington, DC: Regnery Publishing, Inc., 1996.

Gallagher, Maggie. "Fatherless Boys Grow Up Into Dangerous Men." *The Wall Street Journal,* December 1, 1998, p. A22.

Garfinkel, Irwin, Sara S. McLanahan, Daniel R. Meyer, & Judith A. Seltzer, eds. *Fathers under Fire: The Revolution in Child Support Enforcement.* New York: Russell Sage Foundation, 1998.

Garfinkel, Irwin & Marygold S. Melli. "The Use of Normative Standards in Family Law Decisions: Developing Mathematical Standards for Child Support." *Family Law Quarterly,* vol. 24 no. 2, Summer 1990, pp, 157-78.

Gilder, George. *Men and Marriage.* Gretna, LA: Pelican Publishing Company, 1986, 1992.

Goldberg, Steven. *Why Men Rule: A Theory of Male Dominance.* Chicago: Open Court Publishing Company, 1993.

Golden, Lawrence J. *Equitable Distribution of Property.* New York: Shepard's/McGraw-Hill, 1983 & Supps.

Guidubaldi, John, Joseph D. Perry & Bonnie K. Nastasi. "Growing Up in a Divorced Family: Initial and Long-Term Perspectives on Children's Adjustment," in Okamp, S., ed., *Family Processes and Problems: Social Psychological Aspects,* pp. 202-37. Newbury Park, CA: Sage Publications, 1987.

Henry, Ronald K. "'Primary Caretaker': Is It a Ruse?" *Family Advocate,* vol. 17 no. 1, Summer 1994, pp. 53-56.

Hill, Martha S. "The Wage Effects of Marital Status and Children." *The Journal of Human Resources,* vol. 14 no. 4, 1979, pp. 579-94.

Hoffman, Saul D. "Marital Instability and the Economic Status of Women." *Demography,* vol. 14 no. 1, February 1977, pp. 67-76.

Hoffman, Saul D. & Greg J. Duncan. "What Are the Economic Consequences of Divorce?" *Demography,* vol. 25 no. 4, November 1988, pp. 641-45.

Horgan, Timothy J. *Winning Your Divorce,* New York: Dutton, 1994.

Horn, Wade F. *Father Facts,* 3rd ed. Gaithersburg, MD: The National Fatherhood Initiative, 1998.

Horner, Thomas M. & Melvin J. Guyer. "Prediction, Prevention, and Clinical Expertise in Child Custody Cases in Which Allegations of Child Sexual Abuse Have Been Made: I. Predictable Rates of Diagnostic Error in Relation to Various Clinical Decisionmaking Strategies." *Family Law Quarterly,* vol. 25 no. 2, Summer 1991, pp. 217-52.

Horner, Thomas M. & Melvin J. Guyer. "Prediction, Prevention, and Clinical Expertise in Child Custody Cases in Which Allegations of Child Sexual Abuse Have Been Made: II. Prevalence Rates of Child Sexual Abuse and the Precision of 'Tests' Constructed to Diagnose It." *Family Law Quarterly,* vol. 25 no. 3, Fall 1991, pp. 381-409.

Irving, Howard H., Michael Benjamin & Nicolas Trocme. "Shared Parenting: An Empirical Analysis Utilizing a Large Data Base." *Family Process,* vol. 23, 1984, pp. 561-69; republished as "Shared Parenting: An Empirical Analysis Utilizing a Large Canadian Data Base," in Folberg, Jay, ed., *Joint Custody and Shared Parenting,* pp. 128-35. Washington, DC: BNA Books, 1984.

Jacob, Herbert. *Silent Revolution: The Transformation of Divorce Law in the United States.* Chicago: The University of Chicago Press, 1988.

Jacobs, Margaret A. "No Prenup? No Problem: More Couples Sign Postnups." *The Wall Street Journal,* July 21, 1999, pp. B1, B4.

Kammer, Jack. *Good Will Towards Men: Women Talk Candidly about the Balance of Power between the Sexes.* New York: St. Martin's Press, 1994.

Kelly, Joan Berlin. *Examining Resistance to Joint Custody.* Paper presented at Association of Family and Conciliation Courts meeting, San Francisco, May 1982; in Folberg, Jay, ed., *Joint Custody and Shared Parenting,* pp. 39-46. Washington, DC: BNA Books, 1984.

Kelly, Joan Berlin. "Further Observations on Joint Custody." *University of California at Davis Law Review,* vol. 16, 1983, pp. 762-70.

Kelly, Joan Berlin. "The Determination of Child Custody in the USA." *World Wide Legal Information Association,* www.wwlia.org/us-cus.htm, 07/30/97.

Krause, Harry D. "Child Support Reassessed: Limits of Private Responsibility and the Public Interest." *Family Law Quarterly,* vol. 24 no. 1, pp. 1-34, Spring 1990; in Sugarman, Stephan D. & Herma Hill Kay, *Divorce Reform at The Crossroads,* pp. 166-90. New Haven: Yale University Press, 1990.

Kuhn, Richard & John Guidubaldi. *Child Custody Policies and Divorce Rates in the U.S.* Paper presented at 11th Annual Conference of the Children's Rights Council, Washington, DC, October 23-26, 1997.

Lazear, Edward P. & Robert T. Michael. *Allocation of Income within the Household.* Chicago: The University of Chicago Press, 1988.

Levin, Michael. *Feminism and Freedom.* New Brunswick, NJ: Transaction Books, 1987.

Leving, Jeffrey M. & Kenneth A. Dachman. *Fathers' Rights.* New York: Basic Books, 1997.

Levy, David L., ed. *The Best Parent is Both Parents: A Guide to Shared Parenting in the 21st Century.* Norfalk, VA: Hampton Roads Publishing Company, 1993.

Levy, Robert J. "Using 'Scientific' Testimony to Prove Child Sexual Abuse." *Family Law Quarterly,* vol. 23 no. 3, Fall 1989, pp. 383-409.

"Marital Problems, Not Drugs, Seen As Biggest Burden on Productivity." *Behavior Today,* vol. 21 no. 8, February 19, 1990, pp. 1-3.

Marlow, Lenard & Richard S. Sauber. *The Handbook of Divorce Mediation.* New York: Plenum Press, 1990.

Mauet, Thomas A. *Fundamentals of Trial Technique,* 2nd ed. Boston: Little, Brown and Company, 1988.

McElhaney, James W. *McElhaney's Trial Notebook,* 2nd ed. Chicago: Section of Litigation, American Bar Association, 1987.

McIsaac, Hugh. "*The Divorce Revolution:* A Critique." *California Family Law Report,* vol. 10 no. 5, May 1986, pp. 3069-72.

Medved, Diane. *The Case Against Divorce.* New York: Ivy Books, 1989.

Mendelson, Robert. *A Divided Family: A Divorced Father's Struggle with the Child Support Industry.* Amherst, NY: Prometheus Books, 1997.

Miller, Stuart A. "The Myth of Deadbeat Dads." *The Wall Street Journal,* March 2, 1995, p. A14.

Mnookin, Robert H. & Lewis Kornhauser. "Bargaining in the Shadow of the Law: The Case of Divorce." *The Yale Law Journal,* vol. 88, 1979, pp. 950-997; *Current Legal Problems* 1979, pp. 65-105.

Moskowitz, Lawrence. *Unfair Tactics in Matrimonial Cases.* New York: John Wiley & Sons, 1990 & Supps.

Moss, Debra Cassens. "'Real' Dolls Too Suggestive: Do Anatomically Correct Dolls Lead to False Abuse Charges?" *ABA Journal,* December 1, 1991, pp. 24-25.

Novak, James. *The Wisconsin Father's Guide to Divorce and Custody.* Madison: Prairie Oaks Press, 1996.

Oddenino, Michael. "Helping Your Client Navigate Past the Shoals of a Child Custody Evaluation." *American Journal of Family Law,* vol. 8 no. 2, Summer 1994, pp. 81-95.

Oldham, J. Thomas. *Divorce, Separation and the Distribution of Property.* New York: Law Journal Seminars-Press, 1987 & Supps.

O'Neill, June. "Women and Wages." *The American Enterprise,* November/December 1990, pp. 25-33.

Parker, Kathleen. "A Father's Best Gift? His Presence." *Orlando Sentinel,* www.orlandosentinel.com, 10/03/99.

Pearson, Jessica, Nancy Thoennes & Patricia Tjaden. "Legislating Adequacy: The Impact of Child Support Guidelines." *Law & Society Review,* vol. 23 no. 4, 1989, pp. 569-90.

Peterson, Richard R. "A Re-evaluation of the Economic Consequences of Divorce." *American Sociological Review,* vol. 61, June 1996, pp. 528-36.

Popenoe, David. *Life without Father.* New York: Martin Kessler Books/The Free Press, 1996.

Redman, R. Michael. "The Support of Children in Blended Families: A Call for Change." *Family Law Quarterly,* vol. 25 no. 1, Spring 1991, pp. 83-94.

Reed, Fred. "Against Marriage: Cutting and Running, and Why Taipei Is Better." *Fred on Everything,* www.fredoneverything.com, 08/26/99.

Reidy, Thomas J., Richard M. Silver & Alan Carlson. "Child Custody Decisions: A Survey of Judges." *Family Law Quarterly,* vol. 23 no. 1, Spring 1989, pp. 75-87.

Ricci, Isolina. *Mom's House, Dad's House: Making Shared Custody Work.* New York: Collier Books, 1980.

Riley, Glenda. *Divorce: An American Tradition.* New York: Oxford University Press, 1991.

Robinson, Holly L. "Joint Custody: An Idea Whose Time Has Come." *Journal of Family Law,* vol. 21, 1982-83, pp. 641-85.

Robinson, John P. "Caring for Kids." *American Demographics,* July 1989, p. 52.

Roman, Mel & William Haddad. *The Disposable Parent: The Case for Joint Custody.* New York: Holt, Rinehart and Winston, 1978.

Salfi, Dominick J. & Virginia Cassady. "'Prenups': A New Test for Enforceability." *The Florida Bar Journal,* February 1989, pp. 41-43.

Sandmire, Michael J. & Michael Wald. "Licensing Parents–A Response to Claudia Mangel's Proposal." *Family Law Quarterly,* vol. 24 no. 1, Spring 1990, pp. 53-76.

Saposnek, Donald. *Mediating Child Custody Disputes.* San Francisco: Jossey-Bass Publishers, 1983.

Saxe, David B. "Dinosaur Tales." *ABA Journal,* January 1994, pp. 52-54.

Seidenberg, Robert & William Dawes. *The Father's Emergency Guide to Divorce-Custody Battle.* Takoma Park, MD: JES Books, 1997.

Seltzer, Judith A. "Father by Law: Effects of Joint Legal Custody on Nonresident Fathers' Involvement with Children." *Demography,* vol. 35 no. 2, May 1998, pp. 135-46.

Smith, James P. & Michael Ward. "Women in the Labor Market and in the Family." *Journal of Economic Perspectives,* vol. 3 no. 1, Winter 1989, pp. 9-23.

Sommers, Christina Hoff. *Who Stole Feminism? How Women Have Betrayed Women.* New York: Simon & Schuster, 1994.

Stone, Lawrence. *Road to Divorce: England 1530-1987.* Oxford: Oxford University Press, 1990.

Stroup, Atlee L. & Gene L. Pollock. "Economic Consequences of Marital Dissolution." *Journal of Divorce & Remarriage (The Haworth Press, Inc.)* vol. 22 no. 1/2, 1994, pp. 37-54.

The State of Our Unions 1999: The Social Health of Marriage in America. New Brunswick, NJ: The National Marriage Project, Rutgers, The State University of New Jersey, 1999.

Tucker, William. "America's Drift Toward Polygamy." *The Family in America,* vol. 1 no. 10, December 1987, pp. 1-8.

Turner, Brett R. *Equitable Distribution of Property,* 2nd ed. New York: Shepard's/McGraw-Hill, 1994 & Supps.

U.S. Bureau of the Census, Current Population Reports, Series P-23 No. 167, *Child Support and Alimony: 1987,* by Gordon H. Lester, U.S. Government Printing Office, Washington, DC, 1990.

U.S. Bureau of the Census, Current Population Reports, Series P-60 No. 173, *Child Support and Alimony: 1989,* by Gordon H. Lester, U.S. Government Printing Office, Washington, DC, 1991.

U.S. Bureau of the Census, Current Population Reports, Series P-60 No. 187, *Child Support for Custodial Mothers and Fathers: 1991 (Draft),* Washington, DC, 1995.

U.S. Bureau of the Census, Current Population Reports, Series P-60 No. 196, *Child Support for Custodial Mothers and Fathers: 1995,* by Lydia Scoon-Rogers, Washington, DC, 1995.

U.S. Bureau of the Census, Current Population Reports, Series P-20 No. 514, *Marital Status and Living Arrangements: March 1998 (Update),* by Terry A. Lugaila, Washington, DC, 1998.

U.S. General Accounting Office, Report to the Secretary-designate of Health and Human Services, *Child Support Assurance: Effect of Applying State Guidelines to Determine Fathers' Payments,* Washington, DC, January, 1993.

Walker, Glynnis. *Solomon's Children: Exploding the Myths of Divorce.* New York: Arbor House, 1986.

Ware, Ciji. *Sharing Parenthood After Divorce.* Toronto: Bantam Books, 1984.

Warshak, Richard A. *The Custody Revolution.* New York: Poseidon Press, 1992.

Whitehead, Barbara Dafoe. *The Divorce Culture.* New York: Alfred A. Knopf, 1997.

Wilkie, Jane Riblett. *The Decline in Men's Labor Force Participation and Income and the Changing Structure of Family Support in the United States.* Storrs, CT: Institute for the Study of Women and Gender, University of Connecticut, 1990.

Williams, Frank S. *Child Custody and Parental Cooperation.* Paper Presented at American Bar Association Family Law Section, August 1987; *Joint Custodian,* 1988.

Young, Cathy. *Ceasefire! Why Women and Men Must Join Forces to Achieve Equality.* New York: The Free Press, 1999.